THE NEW EMMERDALE COOKBOOK

THE NEW
EMMERDALE
COOKBOOK

Recipes by
Christine France

Text by
Karen Grimes

GRANADA
MEDIA

First published in Great Britain in 1999
by Granada Media
an imprint of André Deutsch Limited
in association with Granada Media Group
76 Dean Street
London
W1V 5HA
www.vci.co.uk

A catalogue record for this book is
available from the British Library.

ISBN 0 233 99717 2

Designed by Roger Hammond

Printed in the UK by Jarrold Book Printing

1 3 5 7 9 10 8 6 4 2

Contents

Introduction

WELCOME TO *THE NEW EMMERDALE COOKBOOK*. As the title suggests, this is more than a traditional country recipe book. The dishes included reflect a newer, fresher feel about the village, its inhabitants and their way of living, working and eating. It's a culinary celebration of the variety of life in Emmerdale!

People from all walks of life have contributed their favourite recipes, ranging from the traditional and the quick-and-easy to the downright extravagant and sophisticated. They reflect the eclectic nature of the village of Emmerdale, although, true to their location, many recipes make full use of the countryside's abundance of fresh meat, fruit and vegetables. Dishes range in their degree of difficulty, so everyone can have a go. If you can't master Marlon's Caramel Croquembouche Tower at the first attempt, try something a little simpler – it'll be just as much fun.

Times change and Emmerdale has changed with them. For instance, many recipes in *The New Emmerdale Cookbook* reflect the foreign flavours brought back to the Dales from the villagers' international travels. This is certainly a far cry from the days when Annie Sugden talked wistfully of her last holiday from the farm –

Bridlington in 1943! Not that the Yorkshire coast has lost its magic. Mandy was quite looking forward to her weekend in Scarborough until Paddy whisked her off to Venice for a romantic Italian escapade.

In fact, the characters one would least expect to have travelled widely have actually contributed the most exotic dishes. The Dingles might be the local ne'er-do-wells of

Emmerdale, but their family connections spread across the globe. In the last couple of years they've caused mayhem in Australia and Italy – and who knows where they might turn up next. Luckily, Marlon's talents have ensured that the memory of these foreign jaunts is preserved in his own special recipes. We've included quite a few quirky dishes, to give you a home-grown taste of the Dingle way of life. Alan Turner, as Emmerdale's resident gastronome, would be expected to make a contribution to any village cookbook, and inside

he offers several mouthwatering suggestions – but with a new twist. Since suffering a mild heart attack Alan has come to realize that good health can be synonymous with good eating, and here he introduces his favourite low-fat recipes. Luckily for Alan, special treats can still be had. Now that Bernice is landlady of the Woolpack, the tradition of gourmet food continues with chef Marlon at the helm. Alan won't have to worry about wasting away to nothing just yet.

The New Emmerdale Cookbook caters for all tastes and for all occasions. Communal events – weddings, Christmas celebrations, cricket matches to name but a few – are all reasons to come together and celebrate with food, drink and laughter. The book includes dishes that are perfect for alfresco summer dining as well as easy-to-fix brunches and lunches for leisurely country mornings. The selection of dinners and main meals is designed to appeal to all tastes, occasions and pockets – from Zak's fiery hot vindaloo, to simple one-pot meals or a classy duck dish from sophisticated Zoe Tate.

And to finish, there are more than enough cakes, bakes and puddings to tempt the palate and terrify the waistline. The recipes contained within are designed to be enjoyed and incorporated into your family's routine – you might even like to try Dingle-style nettle soup for the first time, courtesy of Mandy.

The delicious dishes in The New Emmerdale Cookbook will give you a real taste of Emmerdale life. We do hope you enjoy this culinary tour of the village as much as we have enjoyed making it. So with love from everyone at Emmerdale, please read on and enjoy!

Snacks and Starters

S ince Bernice employed Marlon at the Woolpack, food there has improved immeasurably – even Alan Turner grudgingly acknowledges that it *almost* reaches his own high standards. Alan has always thought of himself as a *bon viveur*, and entertained the villagers for a good while in the Woolpack restaurant. The recipe for Crêpes aux Fruits de Mer comes from the night he treated the Dingles to a gourmet dining experience – and what a night that was! Nellie won the meal in a raffle, and invited thirteen of the clan to sample Alan's finest fare.

Becoming landlady of the Woolpack is Bernice's most precious dream come true. Even the sight of her name spelt incorrectly (Blockstack) on the new sign failed to dampen her joy when Alan handed over the reins. Marlon's sterling efforts at the opening party secured him a regular spot in the Woolpack kitchen, even though Bernice practically made him beg to be allowed to prove himself. They both have very definite ideas about what should and should not be on the menu, and so far the partnership has worked out extremely well. Bernice is succeeding in taking the local pub grub a little more upmarket, and Marlon, whose aim is to open a Marlon's restaurant on every high street in Britain, enjoys the freedom to experiment he never had at the diner. As he said to Alan at the handover party, 'I feel as though I've finally left the desert of burger and chips and moved to the foothills of *haute cuisine*.'

Also included in this chapter are a couple of the most popular quick snacks from the diner, and Marlon will probably take credit for them too! A bit of his talent might even have rubbed off on the rest of the Dingles, as there are a couple of great filling dishes from Butch and Zak in this chapter which should keep hunger pangs at bay.

Roasted Vegetable Terrine

This classy starter created by Marlon for the Woolpack shows the lasting influence of his Italian interlude. It's a real stunner, with all the sunny, intense colours and flavours of the Mediterranean packed into one dish! Marlon added his own inimitable style by making it in a rabbit-shaped mould, but you can pick whatever shape you want.

Serves 6

1 large, long aubergine
2 large courgettes
2 large yellow peppers
2 large red peppers
60ml/4 tablespoons olive oil
2 garlic cloves
300ml/½ pint passata
45ml/3 tablespoons dry
    white wine
15ml/1 tablespoon sherry
    vinegar
10ml/2 teaspoons gelatine
60ml/4 tablespoons
    chopped fresh basil
salt and freshly ground
    black pepper

Marlon's tip
There is no end to my ingenuity. With this dish if you prefer, the vegetables can be brushed with oil and cooked under a hot grill instead of roasted in the oven.

1 Preheat the oven to 220°C/425°F/Gas Mark 7. Trim the aubergine and cut into long, thin slices. Trim the courgettes and cut into long, thin slices. Cut the peppers into quarters and remove the seeds.

2 Lightly oil 2–3 baking sheets and arrange the peppers, aubergine and courgettes in a single layer. Brush with oil. Add the garlic cloves, unpeeled.

3 Bake the vegetables in the oven for 20–25 minutes, turning occasionally, until tender and golden brown. The pepper skins should be charred and blackened and puffed up – if not, return them to the oven for a few more minutes.

4 Remove the vegetables from the oven and cool, then peel off the pepper skins. Slit open the garlic cloves and squeeze out the soft flesh, then stir into the passata.

5 Line a 1.5 litre/2¾ pint loaf tin with clingfilm and brush with oil. Place the wine and vinegar in a small bowl and sprinkle over the gelatine. Leave to soak for 10 minutes, then put the bowl in a pan of simmering water until the gelatine is completely dissolved. Stir into the passata.

6 Arrange the slices of aubergine over the base and sides of the loaf tin. Arrange layers of the courgettes and peppers in the tin, sprinkling with basil, salt and pepper and spooning a little of the passata between each layer. Spoon any remaining passata over the top and fold over the ends of the aubergine. Tap the tin to make sure there are no air bubbles.

7 Chill the terrine in the fridge for 3–4 hours or until set. Turn out the terrine and cut into slices with a sharp serrated knife. Serve with a few rocket leaves and a drizzle of extra virgin olive oil and balsamic vinegar. Serve with crusty bread.

Warm Olive Bruschetta with Chargrilled Peppers and Mozzarella

These colourful little toasts are served in the diner. They're packed with Mediterranean flavours, and make a satisfying starter or snack. Close your eyes and you could be back in Bar Dinglesi!

Serves 4

2 medium red peppers
2 medium yellow peppers
30ml/2 tablespoons extra
   virgin olive oil
30ml/2 tablespoons red
   pesto
300g/10½oz mozzarella
   cheese
salt and freshly ground
   black pepper
1 olive ciabatta loaf
1 garlic clove
25g/1oz pine nuts, toasted
10ml/2 teaspoons balsamic
   vinegar
handful of fresh basil leaves

1 Preheat the grill to very hot. Halve and de-seed the peppers and place skin side upwards on the grill pan. Grill for about 10 minutes, or until the skins are blackened and charred and the peppers are tender. Cool.

2 Peel the skins from the peppers and cut the flesh into 1cm/½in wide strips. Place in a bowl and stir in the oil and pesto. Dice the mozzarella and add with salt and pepper to taste.

3 Slice the ciabatta thickly into about 8 slices, cutting at a diagonal angle to make long slices. Grill for 1–2 minutes on each side until golden brown. Cut the garlic clove in half crosswise, then rub the cut surface generously over the surface of each slice of hot toast.

4 Spoon the pepper and cheese mixture over the toasts and place under the grill for 1–2 minutes, until bubbling. Serve immediately, sprinkled with pine nuts, balsamic vinegar and basil leaves.

Kathy's tip
The pepper mixture can be prepared in advance, then added to the freshly toasted ciabatta just before flashing under the grill to serve.

Alan's tip

If you are preparing for a small soirée, these crêpes can be prepared and filled up to 24 hours in advance, ready for baking when you need them. Cover and store them in the refrigerator, then bake as above.

Alan – dressed as Merlin at the Woolpack's Camelot night – enjoys a pint of Ephraim Monks.

Crêpes aux Fruits de Mer

Alan once declared that his aim was 'to spread a little culinary delight into the humdrum lives' of the Dingles. When they won a gourmet meal at the Woolpack, Alan cooked a lavish French-inspired spread, including these elegant seafood-filled crêpes. Although they enjoyed it, the Dingles were distinctly unhappy about being fed 'foreign muck' – Zak even complained that his Potage de Légumes Froid was cold!

Serves 4

100g/3½oz plain flour
pinch of salt
1 medium egg
300ml/½ pint milk and water
    mixed (ideally ¼ pint of
    each)
butter for frying

FILLING
200g/7oz monkfish fillet
200g/7oz salmon fillet
8 queen scallops
150ml/5fl oz dry white
    wine
strip of lemon zest
200g/7oz cooked peeled
    prawns
15ml/1 tablespoon
    cornflour
250ml/9fl oz milk
15g/½oz butter
salt and freshly ground
    black pepper
60ml/4 tablespoons single
    cream or crème fraîche
15ml/1 tablespoon chopped
    fresh dill
175g/6oz Gruyère cheese,
    grated

1 Sift the flour and salt into a bowl, make a well in the centre and add the egg with a little of the milk and water. Whisk until smooth, then add the remaining milk and whisk to a smooth, bubbly batter.

2 Heat a small knob of butter in a small, heavy-based frying pan. Pour in a little batter and quickly swirl evenly over the pan. Cook until the underneath is golden brown.

3 Either toss or turn the pancake, then cook over a moderate heat until the second side is golden brown. Remove and cook the remaining batter in the same way, making about 8 small pancakes.

4 Preheat the oven to 200°C/400°F/Gas Mark 6. Cut the monkfish and salmon into bite-sized chunks and place in a pan with the scallops, wine and lemon zest. Bring to the boil, then reduce the heat, cover and simmer for 3 minutes. Add the prawns and simmer for 1 minute. Pour off the liquid and reserve.

5 Blend the cornflour with a little of the milk in a small pan, then stir in the remaining milk, the fish liquor and the butter. Whisk over a moderate heat until boiling and thickened. Remove from the heat, season to taste and stir in the cream, dill and fish.

6 Divide the filling equally between the pancakes, roll up and arrange in a wide ovenproof dish, pouring over any spare sauce. Sprinkle with the cheese. Bake in the oven for about 15 minutes, until golden brown and bubbling. Garnish with sprigs of dill.

Thai Crab Cakes with Chilli Peanut Dip

Marlon created this sophisticated starter for the new Woolpack menu. He learnt a lot about Eastern cooking from Dee, and this dish also suits Bernice's worldly tastes – chilli peanut dips are certainly a step up from bowls of bar snacks!

Serves 4

200g/7oz white fish fillet (e.g. cod or haddock) without skin
15ml/1 tablespoon Thai fish sauce (nam pla)
15ml/1 tablespoon Thai red curry paste
15ml/1 tablespoon lime juice
1 garlic clove, crushed
1 egg white
170g can crabmeat
4 dried kaffir lime leaves, crushed
30ml/2 tablespoons chopped fresh coriander
salt and freshly ground black pepper
flour for shaping
oil for shallow frying

PEANUT DIP
1 small fresh red chilli
15ml/1 tablespoon dark soy sauce
15ml/1 tablespoon lime juice
15ml/1 tablespoon soft light brown sugar
45ml/3 tablespoons chunky peanut butter
60ml/4 tablespoons coconut milk

1 Put the fish fillet into a food processor with the fish sauce, curry paste, lime juice, garlic and egg white. Process to a smooth paste.

2 Drain the crabmeat thoroughly and mix with the fish paste, lime leaves and coriander. Mix thoroughly to distribute the ingredients evenly. Lightly flour your hands and shape the mixture into 8–12 small, round patties.

3 For the dip, halve and de-seed the chilli, then chop finely. Place in a small pan with the remaining ingredients and heat gently, stirring constantly, until well blended. Adjust the seasoning to taste.

4 Shallow fry the crab cakes in batches for 3–4 minutes each side, until golden brown. Drain on absorbent kitchen paper and serve hot on a bed of green salad leaves, with the chilli peanut dip.

Marlon's tip
Wash your hands thoroughly after de-seeding and chopping the chilli, as the juices can cause an unpleasant burning effect, especially in the eyes.

Nettle Soup with Onions

Food for free always appeals to the Dingles, and nettles are something Mandy is used to cooking – she once cooked Trotter Broth followed by Boiled Tripe in Nettle and Onion Sauce to impress Paddy! This fresh, green, delicious soup is a rather more palatable way to cook with nettles.

Serves 6

25g/1oz butter
2 medium onions, chopped
100g/3½oz young nettle tops
300g/10½oz potatoes, peeled and diced
500ml/18fl oz chicken stock
large sprig of fresh thyme
salt and freshly ground black pepper
500ml/18fl oz milk
freshly grated nutmeg

1 Melt the butter in a large, heavy-based pan and add the onions. Fry gently, stirring, for 2–3 minutes, then add the nettle tops and potatoes.

2 Reduce the heat, cover tightly with a lid and cook very gently, shaking the pan occasionally to prevent browning or sticking, for about 15 minutes.

3 Add the stock, thyme, salt and pepper. Bring to the boil, then simmer for about 5 minutes or until the potatoes are tender. Remove the sprig of thyme. Purée in a food processor or blender, or press through a sieve.

4 Pour the purée back into the pan and add the milk. Heat until almost boiling, then sprinkle with nutmeg and adjust the seasoning to taste. Serve with crusty bread.

 Mandy's tips
For the best flavour and colour, pick the young nettle tops in midsummer, before the nettles go to seed. Watch your fingers though. For an extra tasty touch, finely dice a couple of rashers of streaky bacon and fry until crisp, then scatter over the soup just before serving.

Butch's Porky Pasties

These satisfying pork-filled pasties are ideal for big lads with hearty appetites. They taste especially good when eaten outdoors, and they're just as good hot or cold – great for impromptu lunchtime picnics with Emily.

Serves 4

**350g/12oz lean pork
    sausagemeat**
5ml/1 teaspoon dried sage
**2 rashers smoked bacon,
    diced**
1 small leek, diced
1 dessert apple, diced
**10ml/2 teaspoons
    wholegrain mustard**
**salt and ground black
    pepper**
**350g/12oz frozen shortcrust
    pastry, thawed**
beaten egg to glaze

1 Preheat the oven to 200°C/400°F/Gas Mark 6. Mix the sausagemeat with the sage and roll into bite-sized balls. Mix with the bacon, leek, apple and mustard. Season with salt and pepper.

2 Divide the pastry dough into 4. Roll out each piece on a lightly floured work surface to a round approximately 3mm/⅛in thick. Using a 19cm/7½in upturned plate as a guide, cut around the plate with a sharp knife to make 4 pastry rounds.

3 Divide the filling mixture between the rounds. Brush all around the edge of each round with beaten egg, then lift the edges up over the filling. Pinch the edges together and crimp to form a seam over the top.

4 Lift the pasties on to a baking sheet and brush with beaten egg to glaze. Bake for about 20 minutes, then lower the heat to 180°C/350°F/Gas Mark 4 for a further 30 minutes to cook the filling.

 Butch's tip
Tastes even better when made with our pigs – but not my Emily, my little piglet. I named her after the real Emily. She's me favourite.

Viv was outraged when Butch brought his favourite piglet Emily into the shop to introduce her to his favourite girl, Emily. Butch names all his pigs after the women in his life, the romantic old so-and-so!

Heartwarming Vegetable Soup

Sometimes true love needs a helping hand, and Betty's special 'heartwarming' soup provided the perfect catalyst for shy lovers Butch and Emily. Packed with tasty vegetables, its warm, rich flavour will warm any heart on a cold day!

Serves 4–6

175g/6oz onion
250g/9oz carrots
200g/7oz parsnips
200g/7oz swede
2 sticks celery
15ml/1 tablespoon
    sunflower oil
15g/½oz butter
1 litre/1¾ pints chicken or
    vegetable stock
55g/2oz green lentils
30ml/2 tablespoons
    Worcestershire sauce
15ml/1 tablespoon tomato
    purée
10ml/2 teaspoons dried
    mixed herbs
celery salt and ground
    black pepper
30ml/2 tablespoons
    chopped fresh parsley

1 Peel or trim all the vegetables and cut into 5mm/¼in dice. Heat the oil and butter in a large, heavy-based pan and add the vegetables.

2 Fry, stirring, over a high heat for 2–3 minutes, then reduce the heat, cover and leave the vegetables to 'sweat' over a fairly low heat for 10 minutes, stirring occasionally until softened but not browned.

3 Add the stock, lentils, Worcestershire sauce, tomato purée, herbs, celery salt and pepper. Bring to the boil, then reduce the heat, cover and simmer gently for 35–40 minutes, stirring occasionally, until tender.

4 Adjust the seasoning and stir in the parsley. Serve with crusty bread.

Betty's tip
Seth and I like a nice chunky soup, but if you prefer a smoother soup, purée it in a food processor or with a hand blender for just a few seconds, leaving some texture in the vegetables.

Zak's Steak and Onion Butties

When Zak was courting Lisa he made her a meal – the best rump steak, covered in oil and left to boil for as long as possible! His steak and onion butties are a better bet, however. Possibly the tastiest butties in the Dales, they're certainly a hefty snack with a real flavour kick – Zak's not one for skimping on anything when he's doing the cooking!

Serves 4

4 x 250g/9oz sirloin steaks, about 1cm/½in thick
salt and freshly ground black pepper
8 thick slices crusty bread
25g/1oz butter, softened
20ml/4 teaspoons whole-grain mustard with beer
8 large pickled onions

1 Preheat the grill to very hot. Trim the steaks and snip the edges at intervals to prevent them curling up during cooking. Season on both sides with salt and pepper.

2 Grill the steaks for 3–4 minutes on each side. Meanwhile, thinly spread the butter over the bread slices. Spread a layer of mustard over 4 of the slices. Slice the pickled onions.

3 Place each grilled steak on a mustard-spread slice of bread and top with slices of onion. Top with the remaining bread slices and press down firmly. Serve immediately.

Zak's tip
Eat with both hands!

Dee tried her hardest to broaden Betty's horizons, although Betty held steadfastly to her belief in the superiority of 'plain English cooking'.

Spicy Ginger Chicken Soup with Noodles

Eric's Filipino wife Dee introduced a more exotic flavour to the village and this delicious Filipino-style soup was her mother's recipe. Dee taught Eric how to cook with garlic and ginger, even though Betty insisted that ginger should only ever be used in cakes!

Serves 4

200g/7oz skinless chicken
    breast
1 garlic clove, crushed
15ml/1 tablespoon grated
    fresh ginger
30ml/2 tablespoons Thai
    fish sauce (nam pla)
2 lemon grass stalks
3 kaffir lime leaves
850ml/1½ pints chicken stock
15ml/1 tablespoon
    groundnut oil
4 shallots, finely chopped
juice of 1 lime
1 small fresh red chilli, thinly
    sliced
250ml/9fl oz coconut milk
100g/3½oz cellophane rice
    noodles
3 spring onions, finely
    chopped
salt and freshly ground
    black pepper
30ml/2 tablespoons chopped
    fresh coriander

1 Slice the chicken very thinly into strips, cutting across the grain of the meat. Place in a non-metallic bowl and add the garlic, ginger and fish sauce, tossing to coat the chicken evenly. Cover and chill to marinate for at least 3–4 hours.

2 Roughly chop the lemon grass, then place in a pan with the lime leaves. Add the chicken stock and bring to the boil. Cover and simmer gently for 15 minutes. Strain, reserving the stock.

3 Heat the oil in a large pan and fry the shallots for 4–5 minutes, until softened and golden brown. Add the lime juice and chilli, then stir in the chicken with its marinade, reserved stock and coconut milk.

4 Bring to the boil, then cover and simmer gently for 10 minutes. Break the noodles into short pieces and add to the soup with the spring onions. Simmer for a further 4–5 minutes. Adjust the seasoning to taste with salt and pepper, stir in the coriander and serve.

 Eric's tip
For a fine, precise presentation, the chicken breast will be easier to slice very thinly if it's semi-frozen until just firm.

Skinnydippers with Cajun Dip

Deep-fried potato skins are an eternal favourite with the younger clientele of Kathy's Diner. Kathy spices up the spuds by serving them with an irresistible Cajun dip.

Serves 4

4 large baking potatoes
1 small fresh green chilli
1 small tomato
2.5ml/½ teaspoon celery salt
2 garlic cloves, crushed
100ml/3½fl oz natural
   yogurt
60ml/4 tablespoons
   mayonnaise
freshly ground black pepper
oil for deep frying

1 Scrub the potatoes and prick the skins, then cook in the microwave on High (100% power) for 14–16 minutes, until just tender. Alternatively, bake in the oven at 200°C/400°F/Gas Mark 6 for 1¼–1½ hours. Cool.

2 Cut each potato into 4 wedges and scoop out the flesh from the centre, leaving about 5mm/¼in layer on the skins. Keep the flesh to use in another recipe.

3 To make the dip, chop the chilli and tomato very finely. Mix with the celery salt and garlic, then stir in the yogurt and mayonnaise. Adjust the seasoning to taste.

4 Heat the oil in a deep-frying pan to 190°C/375°F, or until a small piece of potato sizzles and rises to the surface immediately. Fry the potato skins for 4–6 minutes, or until golden brown and crisp.

5 Drain on absorbent kitchen paper and serve hot, with the dip.

Kathy's tip
For lower-fat potatoes, brush the skins lightly with oil and grill or bake until golden and crisp, instead of deep-frying. If you don't want your dip to be too fiery-hot, discard the seeds from the chilli before using, or use a dash of chilli sauce instead.

Tiger Prawns with Garlic and Lime Butter

Marlon was keen to impress Bernice with his catering for her first day as landlady of the Woolpack, and a quick, sophisticated starter like this is ideal for the new pub menu. It takes only minutes to cook, and is best cooked just before serving.

Serves 4

20–24 raw tiger prawns
15ml/1 tablespoon olive oil
40g/1½oz butter
2 shallots, finely chopped
1 garlic clove, finely
    chopped
finely grated zest and juice
    of 1 lime
salt and freshly ground
    black pepper
30ml/2 tablespoons
    chopped fresh basil
lime wedges to serve

1 Peel the prawns, leaving the tail end attached. Heat the oil and butter in a wide, heavy frying pan and fry the shallots and garlic over a moderate heat for 4–5 minutes, until softened and golden brown.

2 Stir in the prawns and cook over a fairly high heat for 2 minutes until just turned pink. Stir in the lime zest and juice and simmer for a further minute, stirring.

3 Season to taste and stir in the basil just before serving with lime wedges.

Bernice's tip

Although Marlon assures me he knows what he's doing, I'm of the opinion that this recipe is also very suitable for scallops – replace the prawns with medium-sized fresh scallops and cook as above.

Despite Bernice's efforts to take the Woolpack upmarket, Roy, Seth and the local lads will ensure it remains a firm favourite for stag nights and drinking sessions. Roy elected to hold his stag night in the pub – but while he was suffering from last-minute nerves the lads hot-footed it to Hotten and gatecrashed Kelly's hen night.

Brunches and Lunches

These dishes are quick and easy any time foods from all corners of the village. Seth demonstrates a fresh way to cook his prize home-grown marrows and Emily places a new twist on that most traditional of northern foods, the black pudding. There is a low-fat omelette from Alan – no excuse to call him Tubby Turner any more – and having retired from the Woolpack he can spend leisurely mornings enjoying a well-prepared brunch.

When Kathy bought the tearooms and wine bar outright from the dastardly Eric Pollard, she decided to totally revamp the interior to reflect the broader outlook of the newly christened Kathy's Diner. She chose a jaunty American theme which has proved very popular in the village, although Betty had a few teething problems with the new lingo. When Scott Windsor ordered a toasted tuna melt on granary with dill pickle on the side and no mayo, poor Betty thought he was speaking double Dutch! The diner has contributed a popular mid-morning dish, its American-style banana pecan pancakes. Eric himself proved the perfect inspiration for the wild mushroom risotto with a hint of menace.

Even the Dingles have an air of sophistication these days. The mixed-grill-in-the-hole recipe is a nod to tradition, but Lisa's quiche is quite a departure. The ever-effervescent

Mandy contributes an Eastern-influenced dish she impressed Alan and Terry with during one of her many spells behind the bar of the Woolpack, and Marlon perfectly combines the tastes of the Mediterranean and the Dales with his Bar Dinglesi special, bacon and egg pizza.

On a more down-to-earth level, those warring families the Sugdens and the Windsors contribute two quick and easy storecupboard meals. They have been at each other's throats ever since Andy Hopwood came to stay with the Sugdens. Viv led a campaign to get Andy removed from school and the sad events of Christmas 1998, when Andy's errant father Billy killed Vic on Christmas Day, only hardened her antagonism, especially towards Sarah. If only they could take a look at themselves they might see that they have more in common than they think!

Lisa's Creamy Bacon and Broccoli Quiche

Belle's christening was a very special occasion, and Lisa broke with years of Dingle tradition when she served up this dish instead of Dingle Stew. The rest of the family even accused her of being middle-class! She had never, ever made anything as fancy as a quiche (pronounced 'kwitch') before, but it was surprisingly easy – it worked out so well, she's thinking of making it again!

Serves 4–6

200g/7oz plain flour
pinch of salt
100g/3½oz butter or block
   margarine
30ml/2 tablespoons cold
   water
175g/6oz small broccoli
   florets
4 rashers lean streaky
   bacon, chopped
4 spring onions, chopped
145g packet of cream cheese
   with garlic and herbs
2 large eggs
150ml/¼ pint milk
45ml/3 tablespoons single
   cream
salt and freshly ground
   black pepper
25g/1oz grated Cheddar
   cheese

1 Preheat the oven to 200°C/400°F/Gas Mark 6. Sift the flour and salt into a bowl. Rub the fat into the flour until the mixture looks like fine breadcrumbs. Gradually add enough cold water to form a firm dough.

2 Roll out the pastry and use to line a 23cm/9in flan tin on a baking sheet. Bake blind for 10 minutes, then remove the beans and paper and bake for a further 5 minutes.

3 Meanwhile, cook the broccoli in boiling water for 5 minutes. Drain well and arrange in the pastry case. Fry the bacon in its own fat until golden brown, stir in the onions, then scatter over the broccoli.

4 Beat together the cheese, eggs, milk and cream. Season well with salt and pepper and pour into the pastry case. Sprinkle the grated Cheddar on top.

5 Bake in the oven at 190°C/375°F/Gas Mark 5 for 25–30 minutes, or until set and golden brown. Serve warm or cold.

Lisa's tip

You've got to be pretty careful when cooking fancy dishes like this. If I've got time in between running the garage, looking after Belle and keeping an eye on Zak, I'll stick the pastry in the fridge for about 30 minutes after lining the tin and before baking. This helps to prevent it shrinking from the tin during baking.

Farmer's Black Pudding Slices with Red Onion Relish

Butch and Emily must be Emmerdale's most romantic couple. Who could doubt the depth of Butch's devotion – not only did he rescue Emily and her father from a car crash, but he promised to eat anything she could make for him – even black pudding and raspberry jam sandwiches! The idea is not really as weird as it first sounds, as the richness of black pudding is balanced well by contrasting sweet, fruity flavours. This red onion relish may be more acceptable to most tastes, but try the raspberry jam instead if you wish!

Serves 4

1 large red onion
1 small eating apple
40g/1½oz butter
45ml/3 tablespoons cranberry sauce
15ml/1 tablespoon raspberry vinegar
salt and freshly ground black pepper
15ml/1 tablespoon sunflower oil
350g/12oz black pudding, sliced
4 thick slices crusty bread
15ml/1 tablespoon English mustard

1 Peel and thinly slice the onion. Peel, core and coarsely grate the apple. Melt 25g/1oz butter and fry the onion over a moderate heat, stirring occasionally, for 5–6 minutes, to soften.

2 Add the apple and cook, stirring, for a further 5 minutes without browning. Stir in the cranberry sauce and raspberry vinegar. Cook over a low heat, stirring occasionally, for 6–8 minutes until thick and soft. Season to taste with salt and pepper.

3 Heat the oil in a heavy frying pan and fry the black pudding slices over a moderate heat until thoroughly heated, turning once.

4 Meanwhile, toast the bread lightly on both sides until golden brown. Spread with the remaining butter, then with mustard, and arrange the black pudding on top. Top with a generous spoonful of the onion relish and serve hot.

Right: The Dingles once applied to the local tourist board to have their farm registered as bed & breakfast accommodation. Not surprisingly, the inspector rejected them, declaring 'we do not have a category adequate to describe your home!'

Wild Mushroom Risotto

Eric Pollard has a reputation as a ladykiller – in more ways than one. This favourite recipe is ideal when 'having a lady for dinner' – it's possible that when the need arises, he could slip in the odd poisonous mushroom without suspicion!

Serves 4

1 medium red onion
2 sticks of celery
1 garlic clove
125g/4½oz shitake
 mushrooms
125g/4½oz oyster
 mushrooms
30ml/2 tablespoons olive oil
25g/1oz butter
250g/9oz Italian carnaroli or
 arborio risotto rice
150ml/5fl oz dry white
 wine
700ml/1¼ pints chicken stock
1 sprig of fresh thyme
finely grated zest of 1
 lemon
salt and freshly ground
 black pepper
handful of fresh thyme
 leaves

1 Peel and thinly slice the onion and celery, and crush the garlic. Wipe and slice the mushrooms.

2 Heat the oil with half the butter in a large, heavy-based pan and sauté the onion and celery for 2–3 minutes, to soften but not brown. Stir in the garlic and mushrooms and cook for a further 2–3 minutes, until softened but not browned.

3 Add the rice and stir for about 1 minute to coat with oil. Stir in the wine, simmer for 2–3 minutes until absorbed, then gradually add a little of the stock. Add the thyme and simmer, stirring, adding more stock as it is absorbed, for a further 15–20 minutes, until the rice is just tender.

4 Stir in the lemon zest and remaining butter, with salt and pepper to taste. Serve the risotto sprinkled with thyme.

Eric's tip

Don't wash the rice before cooking, or you will wash away some of the starch which gives it that wonderfully creamy texture. It's also important to stir the risotto continuously for the right consistency, adding the stock gradually as you stir.

Eric had his eye on Stella's purse as soon as she moved into Home Farm, and attempted to charm her with intimate lunches in expensive restaurants. His plan worked initially but luckily Stella eventually got the measure of him, and when she left the village she also left Eric with some pretty hefty bills to cover!

Alan's Brunch-Lunch Omelette

Alan Turner's favourite pastime has always been gourmet food and fine wine. The combination of over-indulgence and job stress, however, led to him suffering a mild heart attack in April 1999. Luckily granddaughter Tricia is now on hand to make sure that he looks after himself. If, like Alan, you have to watch your fat and cholesterol intake, this light-as-air omelette is the one for you.

Serves 1

100g/3½oz asparagus spears
3 cherry tomatoes, halved
15ml/1 tablespoon chopped
　fresh chervil or parsley
salt and freshly ground
　black pepper
2.5ml/½ teaspoon olive oil
3 egg whites
chopped fresh chervil or
　parsley to serve

1 Trim the asparagus and cut into 3cm/1¼in lengths. Steam or boil for 6–8 minutes, until just tender. Toss with the tomatoes and chervil and season with salt and pepper.

2 Whisk the egg whites until frothy but not stiff. Heat the oil in a small, heavy or non-stick frying pan and pour in the egg whites, spreading them to cover the whole pan. Arrange the asparagus and tomato mixture on top, then cook over a moderate heat for about 2 minutes, until firm and golden underneath.

3 Slide the omelette gently out of the pan on to a plate. Put the pan over the plate and invert the omelette back into the pan. Cook until set and golden underneath. Turn out on to a plate and serve immediately, sprinkled with chervil or parsley.

Tricia's tip

If, like me, you can't be bothered to stand about for ages cooking, take the eggs out of the fridge half an hour before you need them. While you're sitting down having a cuppa the eggs will come to room temperature and then the whites will whisk a lot better.

Marlon's Pizza Inglese con Pancetta e Uovo (Bacon and Egg Pizza)

They say Venice is for lovers, and this dish is certainly a marriage of two culinary cultures. Marlon couldn't resist working a few British flavours into some classic Italian dishes when he helped out at Bar Dinglesi, and this is one of his most successful concoctions.

Serves 2

350g/12oz strong plain
   flour
2.5ml/½ teaspoon salt
pinch of caster sugar
1 sachet easy-blend dried
   yeast
200ml/7fl oz warm water
30ml/2 tablespoons olive oil
30ml/2 tablespoons tomato
   ketchup
30ml/2 tablespoons pesto
   sauce
4 plum tomatoes, sliced
5 smoked streaky bacon
   rashers, diced
2 medium eggs
½ a small onion, finely
   chopped
15ml/1 tablespoon chopped
   fresh marjoram, or
   5ml/1 teaspoon dried
40g/1½oz mozzarella
   cheese, diced
4 pitted black olives, sliced
freshly ground black pepper

1 Preheat the oven to 220°C/425°F/Gas Mark 7. Brush a baking sheet with a little oil. Sift the flour, salt and sugar into a bowl and stir in the yeast.

2 Make a well in the centre and pour in the water and oil. Using your hands, gradually mix the flour into the liquid to form a fairly soft dough. If it is too dry, add a little more liquid.

3 Knead the dough out on a lightly floured worktop with your hands for 10 minutes, until it is smooth and elastic. If it is too sticky, knead in a little more flour. Alternatively, use a mixer with a dough hook attachment.

4 Roll out the dough with a rolling pin to a 30cm/12in round (or divide into two individual ones). Place on the baking sheet, pressing with your knuckles to make a slightly raised edge.

5 Mix together the ketchup and pesto and spread evenly over the dough. Top with tomato slices and scatter with bacon. Make two indentations in the topping and break an egg into each.

6 Scatter with onion, marjoram, mozzarella and olives. Sprinkle with pepper. Bake the pizza in the oven for 20–25 minutes, until golden brown. Serve hot.

Marlon demonstrates his theory that haute cuisine *is the new rock and roll.*

Marlon's tip

Being from a foreign country, Italian bacon isn't like home-reared Dingle bacon. This could be a good thing as you can guarantee Butch hasn't had his mucky fingers on it. I used their pancetta, which is the nearest thing available in Venice – but you should use smoked streaky, as this gives the most genuine British flavour.

Viv regaled Kelly and her friends with tales of her own hen night before her wedding to Vic – dancin'
herself dizzy to 'Blockbuster' by the Sweet at Ritzy's, the top spot in Dagenham.

Quickie Corned Beef and Tomato Frittata

There have been a lot of comings and goings at the village post office in the past year or so. With a constantly squabbling family and a business to run, Viv finds it difficult to plan ahead for meals. This is a speedy, economical one-pan dish using ingredients readily available in the village shop – and it's easily adaptable for between 1 and 4 portions, depending on who's willing to come home for lunch!

Serves 4

350g/12oz cooked or canned
   potatoes
200g can corned beef
1 medium red onion
30ml/2 tablespoons olive oil
125g/4½oz cherry
   tomatoes, halved
4 large eggs, beaten
salt and freshly ground
   black pepper
40g/1½oz mature Cheddar
   cheese, grated
chopped fresh parsley to
   garnish

1 Cut the potatoes and corned beef into 2cm/¾in chunks. Peel and thinly slice the onion.

2 Heat the oil in a large, heavy-based frying pan and fry the onion and potatoes for 3–4 minutes until lightly browned. Add the corned beef and tomatoes.

3 Beat the eggs with the salt and pepper, then pour over the ingredients in the pan. Cook over a moderate heat for 3–4 minutes, until golden brown underneath and just set on top.

4 Sprinkle the cheese over the top and place under a hot grill for 1–2 minutes, until bubbling and golden brown. Sprinkle with parsley, cut into wedges and serve hot.

Viv's tip
If little madam Kelly's in a strop, this frittata can also be served cold – cool after cooking, then store in the fridge and cut into slices to serve just as it is.

Dingle Special Mixed Grill-in-the-Hole

This meaty brunch-style version of toad-in-the-hole feeds a hungry bunch and has a special Dingle batter – the addition of lager really works to make it crisp and light. Lisa uses Zak's favourite brew, Ephraim Monks, but you can use your usual tipple.

Serves 4

15ml/1 tablespoon
   sunflower oil
4 pork sausages
4 lamb kidneys
4 lamb cutlets
4 thick rashers back bacon
1 medium onion, sliced
250g/9oz plain flour
salt and freshly ground
   black pepper
4 medium eggs
200ml/7fl oz milk
250ml/9fl oz lager
5ml/1 teaspoon grated
   horseradish

1 Preheat the oven to 220°C/425°F/Gas Mark 7. Brush a wide baking tin or ovenproof dish with the oil. Arrange the meats in one layer in the tin, add the onion slices and bake in the oven for 10-15 minutes.

2 Meanwhile, sift the flour and seasonings into a bowl and make a well in the centre. Break the eggs into the well and add the milk. Gradually mix in the flour, to make a thick batter. Add the lager and horseradish and beat well to a frothy batter.

3 Reduce the oven temperature to 200°C/400°F/Gas Mark 6. Pour the batter into the hot tin over the meats and return it straight back to the oven. Bake for 35–40 minutes or until the batter is well risen and golden brown. Serve hot, with fresh seasonal vegetables.

 Lisa's tip
My Zak won't stand for soggy batter. The secret of a crisp, well-risen batter is first to stop him nicking the lager and second to make sure the tin is sizzling hot before pouring the batter into it.

American-style Banana Pecan Pancakes

A wonderful brunch dish from Kathy's Diner, or a special treat for the kids on Pancake Tuesday. They can be served with any fruit, but Betty recommends them with strawberries in the summer for a real treat!

Serves 4

100g/3½oz self-raising flour
2.5ml/½ teaspoon baking
    powder
2.5ml/½ teaspoon ground
    cinnamon
15ml/1 tablespoon light
    muscovado sugar
1 medium egg
150ml/¼ pint milk
3 medium bananas
50g/1¾oz pecan nuts
sunflower oil for frying
60ml/4 tablespoons maple
    syrup

1 Sift the flour, baking powder and cinnamon and stir in the sugar. Make a well in the centre, add the egg and milk and whisk to make a smooth, bubbly batter.

2 Peel and mash 2 of the bananas and chop half the pecan nuts. Stir into the batter. Lightly oil a griddle or heavy frying pan and heat until very hot – test with a drop of batter, which should sizzle immediately.

3 Spoon large tablespoons of the batter on to the griddle and cook for 2–3 minutes, turning once, until golden brown on each side. Use up all the batter, to make 8–10 pancakes.

4 Peel and slice the remaining banana. Lift the pancakes on to warm serving plates and top with banana slices and the remaining pecan nuts. Drizzle with maple syrup and serve hot, with whipped cream or Greek yogurt.

Kathy's tip
This batter is different to other mixes. It doesn't improve when made in advance – once it's mixed, you should use it up quickly if you want your pancakes to be really light.

Mandy's Spice-Girl Stir-Fry

This dish reflects Mandy's exuberant personality – it's colourful, full-flavoured and packs a punch! Try it and you'll 'wannabe' back for more – or else!

Serves 4

2.5cm/1in piece root ginger
1 garlic clove
1 small fresh red chilli
1 large red pepper
1 large yellow pepper
3 spring onions
1 firm, ripe mango
400g/14oz chicken breast
    fillets
30ml/2 tablespoons
    sunflower oil
175g/6oz mangetout
15ml/1 tablespoon tomato
    purée
15ml/1 tablespoon soy
    sauce
45ml/3 tablespoons
    medium sherry
5ml/1 teaspoon sesame oil
salt and freshly ground
    black pepper

1 Finely chop the ginger, garlic and chilli. Halve, core and de-seed the peppers, then slice thinly. Thinly slice the spring onions, cutting diagonally. Peel, stone and thinly slice the mango. Cut the chicken into thin strips.

2 Heat the oil in a wok or large frying pan and fry the ginger, garlic and chilli for about 1 minute. Add the peppers and stir-fry over a moderate heat for about 5 minutes, to soften.

3 Raise the heat to high, add the chicken strips and stir-fry for about 5 minutes, or until golden brown. Add the mangetout and stir-fry for a further minute.

4 Mix together the tomato purée, soy sauce, sherry and sesame oil and stir in. Add the spring onions and mango and stir for 1 minute to heat thoroughly. Adjust the seasoning with salt and pepper and serve.

Mandy's tip
If Betty's supped all the sherry, add a squeeze of lime juice instead.

Mandy was short of brass after Eric Pollard evicted her from her clothes shop in the barn. Luckily Bernice came to the rescue and roped Mandy into playing a busty serving wench at the Woolpack's Camelot night – complete with blackened teeth and foaming flagons of mead.

Baked Stuffed Marrow Rings

Seth's vegetables are his pride and joy, but his prize marrows are probably far too large for this recipe. The younger, tender ones should be snapped up for this, with onions and carrots from the garden. It makes a delicious lunch dish on its own, or can be served as an accompaniment to roast meats.

Serves 6

2 small marrows, about
   500g/1lb 2oz each
40g/1½oz butter
1 onion, finely chopped
2 medium carrots, grated
200g/7oz fresh brown or
   white breadcrumbs
175g/6oz Cheddar cheese,
   grated
30ml/2 tablespoons
   chopped fresh oregano
finely grated rind and juice
   of 1 small lemon
2.5ml/½ teaspoon freshly
   grated nutmeg
salt and freshly ground
   black pepper
1 small egg, beaten
60ml/4 tablespoons stock

1 Preheat the oven to 200°C/400°F/Gas Mark 6. Trim the marrows and cut each one into 6 slices. Scoop out the seeds but do not peel. Grease a wide ovenproof dish or baking tin and arrange the slices in it.

2 Melt the butter and fry the onion for 2 minutes to soften. Add the carrots and stir-fry for 3–4 minutes.

3 Add the breadcrumbs, half the cheese, the oregano, lemon rind and juice, nutmeg, salt and pepper. Mix thoroughly, then stir in the egg, mixing well.

4 Spoon the stuffing mixture into the marrow rings. Sprinkle with the remaining cheese and spoon the stock into the dish. Cover with foil and bake for 30–40 minutes, or until tender, uncovering for the final 10 minutes to brown. Serve hot.

Seth's tip

Not everyone can be a prize gardener. If your marrows are tiddlers you can still follow this recipe by cooking them whole – just cut a lengthwise slice from the top, then scoop out the seeds and fill with the stuffing. The cooking time will vary, depending on size.

Tuna and Sweetcorn Carbonara

With three children and a struggling farm to look after, there's little time or money in the Sugden household for culinary extravagance. This is a speedy store-cupboard pasta meal that Sarah relies on for quick family lunches on busy Saturdays. It's made in a matter of minutes, but is very satisfying and nutritious too.

Serves 4

400g/14oz tagliatelle
15ml/1 tablespoon olive oil
1 small onion, finely chopped
3 large eggs, beaten
30ml/2 tablespoons chopped
    fresh parsley, or
    15ml/1 tablespoon dried
salt and freshly ground
    black pepper
55g/2oz Parmesan cheese,
    grated
185g can tuna chunks in
    brine, drained
325g can sweetcorn, drained

1 Cook the tagliatelle in boiling, lightly salted water for 5–7 minutes, until just tender, or according to directions on the packet.

2 Meanwhile, heat the oil and fry the onion for 2–3 minutes, until softened and golden brown. Beat the eggs with the parsley, salt and pepper, and half the Parmesan.

3 Drain the pasta. Add the tuna and corn to the onion and toss to heat gently. Remove from the heat and add the drained pasta, then quickly add the egg mixture and stir gently until set – the heat of the pasta should be enough to lightly cook the eggs.

4 Remove from the heat and sprinkle with the remaining Parmesan to serve.

Sarah's tip

I find that tagliatelle is particularly good for this dish, as the egg coats the ribbons and cooks easily. The kids love sucking it up off the plate and making a mess, too. If you prefer you can use another pasta shape instead – spaghetti, rigatoni or macaroni are also good choices.

Dinners and Main Meals

I f anyone in Emmerdale has a hearty appetite, it must be the Dingles. In this chapter we have included a recipe for the classic Dingle stew, served at all family functions, such as Mrs Kirk's first visit to her prospective in-laws. Mind you, on that occasion she enjoyed Zak's homebrew a little too much! Stews and casseroles are popular with the Dingle clan, mainly because they are cheap, require the minimum of washing up, and are taught in prison cooking lessons! Lisa is obviously a better cook than Zak's first wife Nellie – she even managed to impress Chris Tate with her cooking, when Lady Tara invited the family to stay at Home Farm after their ceiling collapsed. Going out for dinner with the Dingles will invariably involve as hot a curry as one can stand – Zak doesn't normally like foreign muck, but he doesn't count vindaloo as foreign. Those in the know keep away when he's eaten too much. On one occasion he polished off everyone's leftovers at Hotten Spicy, the local curry house, before declaring that his guts felt as if a herd of wildebeest had been let loose in there! The younger Dingles appear to have developed more sophisticated tastes on their foreign travels – on their Venetian honeymoon, Mandy and Paddy were most impressed with burrida, and Marlon, as one might expect, adapted an Italian recipe in his own inimitable way.

Zak and Mandy kindly offered to put the newlyweds up chez Dingle when Roy's honeymoon plans fell through. Kelly was treated to a greasy fry-up and a gut-burning vindaloo before Chris Tate came to the rescue and paid for a romantic break in Paris.

There are several easy 'one-pot' meals in this chapter which use lots of fresh meat and vegetables. If you're like the Sugdens, without the time, or like Seth and Kelly, without the inclination to juggle several pans on the stove at once, these dishes are for you. Alternatively for a special dinner there are selections from Alan Turner's dinner menu and a lovely choice for a romantic meal for two from Zoe Tate – let's hope you have better luck than she has. She really fell for Frankie Smith, the Tate Haulage driver, but it was not meant to be. Perhaps the new millennium will bring some romance into Zoe's life – she needs it!

Burrida – Italian Fish Stew

When Mandy and Paddy visited Venice for their honeymoon, they couldn't resist trying some of the local dishes. This delicious local dish can be made with whatever fish is available, but stick to the firmer-fleshed types if you want them to hold their shape during cooking.

Serves 6

2kg/4lb 8oz firm-fleshed
   fish, e.g. monkfish,
   snapper, octopus, squid,
   scampi, tiger prawns
1 litre/1¾ pints water
2 bay leaves
12 peppercorns
1 medium onion
2 sticks of celery
1 medium carrot
½ a small fennel bulb
2 garlic cloves
30ml/2 tablespoons olive oil
600g/1lb 5oz plum
   tomatoes, skinned
100ml/3½fl oz dry white
   wine
salt and freshly ground
   pepper
chopped fresh basil

1 Trim the fish by removing any heads, tails, bones and skin. Place in a pan and pour over the water. Add a bay leaf, the peppercorns and a slice from the onion. Bring to the boil, then reduce the heat, cover and simmer gently for 20 minutes. Strain and keep the stock. Cut the fish into large chunks.

2 Finely dice the remaining onion, celery, carrot and fennel. Finely chop the garlic. Heat the oil and fry the vegetables and garlic gently, stirring, until lightly browned.

3 Roughly chop the tomatoes and add to the pan with the remaining bay leaf. Stir in the wine and allow to boil, uncovered, for a few minutes until well-reduced. Stir in the reserved stock and bring to the boil.

4 If you are using octopus or squid, add these first to the pan and simmer gently for 3–4 minutes. Add firm fish such as monkfish next, and simmer for a further 3–4 minutes. Finally, add the other fish and shellfish such as prawns and simmer for 2–3 minutes.

5 Adjust the seasoning to taste, sprinkle generously with chopped basil and serve the stew with crusty bread.

Opposite: Paddy went to Venice by himself when he and Mandy split up, but he vowed to return one day with Mandy. She was thrilled to discover he had chosen Venice as their honeymoon destination.

Mandy's tip
If you can't get your hands on fresh plum tomatoes, use a 400g/14oz can of plum tomatoes instead (which also saves time, as you don't have to skin them!).

Seth's Yorkshire Rabbit Pie

Rabbit is a tender, low-fat meat which is ideal for pies or casseroles. Seth particularly enjoys this tasty rabbit pie, flavoured with fresh vegetables from the garden. Suet pastry sounds like an unhealthy choice, but this one is actually lower in fat than shortcrust, and you can use either beef or vegetable suet.

Serves 4

15ml/1 tablespoon plain
   flour
salt and freshly ground
   black pepper
500g/1lb 2oz diced rabbit
25g/1 oz butter
125g/4½oz streaky bacon,
   diced
1 large onion, chopped
2 medium carrots, diced
2 sticks of celery, sliced
150ml/¼ pint dry sherry
200ml/7fl oz chicken stock
10ml/2 teaspoons English
   mustard
15ml/1 tablespoon
   redcurrant jelly
15ml/1 tablespoon chopped
   fresh thyme, or
   5ml/1 teaspoon dried

PASTRY
200g/7oz self-raising flour
pinch of salt
85g/3oz shredded suet
milk to glaze

1 Preheat the oven to 200°C/400°F/Gas Mark 6. Sprinkle the flour, salt and pepper over the diced rabbit and toss to coat evenly.

2 Melt the butter and fry the rabbit over a moderate heat until golden brown, turning occasionally. Remove and keep to one side. Add the bacon and fry for 1–2 minutes until lightly coloured. Add the onion, carrots and celery and cook for a further 2 minutes, stirring.

3 Stir in the sherry, bring to the boil, then add the stock, mustard, redcurrant jelly and thyme.

4 Arrange the rabbit in a deep pie dish, layering with the vegetables and spooning over the juices.

5 For the pastry, sift the flour and salt into a bowl and stir in the suet. Add enough cold water to just bind to a fairly soft dough. Roll out to cover the pie dish and pinch the edges to seal.

6 Brush the pastry lightly with milk to glaze and bake in the oven for 25–30 minutes, until the pastry is golden brown and crisp. Serve hot.

Seth's tip
Diced rabbit is easier to use, but I prefer to use rabbit joints. If you do too, cook as above until the pastry is golden brown and crisp, then reduce the oven temperature to 180°C/350°F/Gas Mark 4 and cook for a further 15–20 minutes.

Seth is usually seen propping up the other side of the bar, but he didn't miss the opportunity to pull his own pints at the Hollywood night.

Aromatic Moroccan Chicken

Alan Turner loves surprising his dinner guests with fine foods and unusual flavours, and this exotically spiced Moroccan-style chicken dish really fits the bill.

Serves 4

30ml/2 tablespoons olive oil
8 small chicken joints –
    thighs, drumsticks, etc.
4 small onions
4 cardamom pods
5ml/1 teaspoon cumin
    seeds
5ml/1 teaspoon coriander
    seeds
1 piece of star anise
1 cinnamon stick
2.5ml/½ teaspoon turmeric
500ml/18fl oz chicken stock
1 small fresh green chilli,
    sliced
150g/5½oz dried apricots
15g/½oz butter
45ml/3 tablespoons whole
    blanched almonds
pitted green olives
roughly chopped fresh flat-
    leaf parsley to garnish

1 Heat the oil in a large flameproof casserole or pan and fry the chicken joints over a fairly high heat until browned on all sides. Remove from the pan and drain off any excess fat.

2 Peel the onions and cut into quarters, then fry until golden brown. Lightly crush the cardamom, cumin and coriander with a pestle and mortar to just crack them open, but don't grind them finely. Add to the pan with the anise, cinnamon and turmeric and stir for about a minute.

3 Add the chicken joints, stock, chilli and apricots, then bring to the boil. Reduce the heat, cover and simmer gently for 40–45 minutes, until the chicken is tender and thoroughly cooked.

4 Heat the butter in a small pan and fry the almonds quickly, stirring, until golden brown. Scatter over the casserole with the olives and parsley and serve hot, with couscous.

 Alan's tip
If you want to cut down on fat, remove the skin from the chicken before cooking, and grill the almonds instead of frying in butter.

Southern Fried Chicken with Corn Fritters

A classic down-home American favourite from Kathy's Diner. Popular with the Woolpackers, this simple dish is very easy to make, and really finger-licking good!

Serves 4

12 small chicken joints –
drumsticks, wings, etc.
30ml/2 tablespoons plain
flour
10ml/2 teaspoons ground
allspice
5ml/1 teaspoon ground
black pepper
5ml/1 teaspoon garlic salt
5ml/1 teaspoon dried thyme
1 large egg, beaten
125g/4½oz fresh white
breadcrumbs
oil for deep-frying

FRITTERS
100g/3½oz self-raising flour
salt and freshly ground
black pepper
1 egg
150ml/¼ pint milk
200g/7oz canned or frozen
sweetcorn
30ml/2 tablespoons chopped
fresh chives

1 Remove the skin from the chicken joints and place in a large bowl. Mix together the flour, allspice, pepper, garlic salt and thyme. Sprinkle over the chicken joints, tossing to coat evenly.

2 Dip each piece of chicken first in beaten egg, then roll in the breadcrumbs to coat evenly.

3 To make the fritters, place the flour, salt and pepper in a bowl and add the egg and milk. Whisk to a smooth, thick batter, then add the sweetcorn and chives.

4 Lightly oil a griddle or frying pan, heat until very hot, then drop tablespoonfuls of the batter on to it. Cook in batches for 2–3 minutes to brown on one side, then turn and cook for a further 2–3 minutes to brown on the other side. Remove and keep hot.

5 Heat the oil in a large deep-frying pan to a temperature of 170°C/325°F. Fry the chicken pieces in batches for 8–10 minutes, until golden brown and thoroughly cooked. Drain on absorbent kitchen paper and serve with the corn fritters and a green salad.

 Kathy's tip
The chicken can be coated with egg and breadcrumbs earlier in the day, and stored in the fridge ready for cooking when you're ready. Do make sure the chicken is thoroughly cooked, by piercing through the thickest part of the flesh – if there's any trace of pink, cook it for a few minutes longer.

Jester Tricia wiped the smile off Bernice's face at the Camelot night when she read extracts of Bernice's diary to the entire pub. Even the normally genial Alan voiced his displeasure at Tricia's actions.

Puff-Topped Steak and Ale Pies

These richly flavoured, hearty little pies are a popular winter choice in the Woolpack. The filling is best cooked long and slow in the oven, well in advance of making the pies, so that the flavours become richly concentrated and the meat is meltingly tender.

Serves 6

1kg/2lb 4oz stewing beef
25g/1oz butter
15ml/1 tablespoon
    sunflower oil
2 large onions, thinly sliced
2 garlic cloves, crushed
15ml/1 tablespoon light
    muscovado sugar
45ml/3 tablespoons plain
    flour
300ml/½ pint brown ale
150ml/5fl oz beef stock
30ml/2 tablespoons
    Worcestershire sauce
15ml/1 tablespoon tomato
    purée
bouquet garni
salt and freshly ground
    black pepper
425g pack frozen ready-
    rolled puff pastry, thawed
beaten egg to glaze

1 Preheat the oven to 150°C/300°F/Gas Mark 2. Trim the meat and cut into 3cm/1¼in chunks. Heat half the butter and oil in a flameproof casserole and fry the meat in batches over a high heat, stirring, until browned on all sides. Remove and keep hot.

2 Melt the remaining butter and oil and fry the onions for 3–4 minutes until softened, then add the garlic and sugar and continue to cook until they begin to brown and caramelize.

3 Add the meat to the pan, stir in the flour, then add the beer, stock, Worcestershire sauce, tomato purée and bouquet garni. Season with salt and pepper and bring to the boil. Cover the casserole and place in the oven for about 2 hours, until the meat is tender.

4 Raise the oven temperature to 220°C/425°F/Gas Mark 7. Remove the bouquet garni from the beef mixture and divide the meat between 6 individual (250ml/9fl oz) ovenproof dishes.

5 Cut the pastry to cover the dishes, pressing the edges firmly to seal. Brush the pies with beaten egg to glaze and bake for 20–25 minutes, until risen and golden brown. Serve hot, with a green vegetable.

Bernice's tip
My motto is 'prior planning prevents poor performance' and it's something to bear in mind when you're making this dish. It's useful to make the filling in advance and store it in the freezer – spoon it into the individual dishes before freezing so they're ready to top with a pastry lid for cooking.

Country Lamb and Vegetable Cobbler

An economical one-pot meal from the Sugden family – the vegetables can be varied depending on what's in season, and the oaty scone-dumpling topping makes it filling.

Serves 4

500g/1lb 2oz lean boned
    shoulder or neck of lamb
30ml/2 tablespoons
    vegetable oil
1 large onion, diced
2 carrots, diced
2 small turnips, diced
30ml/2 tablespoons paprika
400g can chopped tomatoes
15ml/1 tablespoon tomato
    purée
150ml/¼ pint lamb or beef
    stock
salt and freshly ground
    black pepper
100g/3½oz frozen peas

COBBLER TOPPING
225g/8 oz self-raising flour
100g/3½ oz shredded
    vegetable suet
30ml/2 tablespoons rolled
    porridge oats
cold water to mix
milk to glaze

1 Trim any excess fat from the meat and cut into 3cm/1¼in chunks. Heat the oil in a large flameproof casserole and fry the meat in batches until golden brown on all sides.

2 Add the vegetables and stir over a moderate heat for 2–3 minutes. Add the paprika, tomatoes, purée, stock and seasonings. Cover and simmer over a low heat for 30 minutes. Stir in the peas.

3 Meanwhile, preheat the oven to 180°C/350°F/Gas Mark 4. For the topping, mix together the flour, suet and oats with salt and pepper. Stir in just enough cold water to make a soft dough.

4 Roll out the dough to 2cm/½in thick and cut out about 12 rounds with a biscuit cutter. Arrange the rounds slightly overlapping over the casserole and brush with milk. Bake in the oven for 30–35 minutes, or until the topping is golden brown and firm.

Sarah's Tip
Did you know it's usually cheaper to buy a can of whole tomatoes and chop them yourself, rather than buying ready-chopped ones?

Zak's Hot Pork Vindaloo

This mustard-laced, fiery-hot curry is a favourite of Zak's. He thinks that anything less strong is 'namby-pamby'! Although pork is rarely eaten in India, the classic Goan vindaloo is made with pork, which suits Zak's taste just fine. If you prefer a milder spice, cut down on the mustard seeds and chillies by about half.

Serves 4

MARINADE

5ml/1 teaspoon black
   mustard seed
5ml/1 teaspoon cumin seed
1 medium onion, chopped
4 garlic cloves, crushed
15ml/1 tablespoon grated
   fresh ginger
30ml/2 tablespoons vinegar
2.5ml/½ teaspoon ground
   cinnamon

CURRY

500g/1lb 2oz boneless leg
   of pork
55g/2oz tamarind paste
300ml/½ pint boiling water
45ml/3 tablespoons
   vegetable oil
1 large onion, sliced
5ml/1 teaspoon crushed
   dried red chillies
5ml/1 teaspoon paprika
5ml/1 teaspoon turmeric
5ml/1 teaspoon salt

1 For the marinade, place the mustard and cumin seeds in a heavy-based pan and stir constantly over a moderate heat for 3–4 minutes, until the seeds darken slightly, but do not allow them to burn.

2 Place the roasted seeds in a blender or processor with the onion, garlic, ginger, vinegar and cinnamon. Process to a smooth paste.

3 Cut the pork into 2.5cm/1in pieces, place in a large bowl and add the marinade. Stir to coat the meat evenly in the spice mixture, then cover and chill overnight.

4 Place the tamarind paste in a bowl, pour over the boiling water and leave to soak for 10 minutes. Strain, pressing as much of the pulp into the juices as possible.

5 Heat the oil in a large pan and fry the onion over a moderate heat until golden brown. Stir in the chillies, paprika and turmeric and stir for about a minute.

6 Add the meat and fry, turning occasionally, until lightly browned on all sides. Stir in the tamarind juice. Add the salt, reduce the heat, cover and simmer for about 30 minutes, until the meat is tender. Serve with boiled rice or naan bread.

 Zak's Tip

I've no idea why, but this curry tastes better if you eat it the day after cooking. The wonders of science, eh? Keep it in the fridge and remember to heat it up again properly before serving. If you can't get tamarind paste, add the juice of ½ a lemon instead.

Pasticciata con Arrosto di Manzo al Marlon

When Marlon helped out at Bar Dinglesi in Venice he brought his own individual Dingle touch to this very rich Italian dish called Vincisgrassi, a special type of lasagne. This version is made with a distinctly English flavour – roast beef and beer! It's a dish with lots of ingredients, and lots of flavour, best made for a crowd but you could halve the amounts to make for a smaller number.

Serves 8

RAGÙ

50g/1¾oz butter

50g/1¾oz pancetta or
bacon, finely chopped

1 onion, finely chopped

1 carrot, finely chopped

1 stick of celery, finely
chopped

200g/7oz chicken livers,
chopped

200ml/7fl oz brown ale

100ml/3½fl oz beef stock

30ml/2 tablespoons tomato
purée

salt and freshly ground
black pepper

FILLING

500g/1lb 2oz fresh spinach
leaves

4 large courgettes

15ml/1 tablespoon olive oil

1 large onion, thinly sliced

1 garlic clove, crushed

100g/3½oz porcini
mushrooms

500g/1lb 2oz fresh lasagne
sheets

350g/12oz thinly sliced
roast beef

400ml/14fl oz passata

350g/12oz Cheddar cheese,
grated

2.5ml/½ teaspoon freshly
grated nutmeg

60ml/4 tablespoons grated
Parmesan cheese

1 For the ragù, melt the butter in a large pan and fry the pancetta or bacon, onion, carrot and celery over a moderate heat, stirring until golden brown. Stir in the chicken livers and cook until lightly browned.

2 Add the beer, stock and tomato purée. Bring to the boil, cover and simmer for 30 minutes. Preheat the oven to 180°C/350°F/ Gas Mark 4.

3 Wash the spinach and drain off excess water, then cook in an open pan over a high heat, turning often, until just wilted with no free liquid. Trim and thinly slice the courgettes lengthwise and cook in boiling water for 2 minutes. Drain.

4 Heat the oil and fry the onion and garlic over a moderate heat until tender and golden brown. Add the mushrooms and cook for 2–3 minutes.

5 Arrange lasagne sheets over the base of a wide, deep tin or straight-sided baking dish. Spread over a third of the ragù, then arrange a layer of courgettes, beef slices, onions and mushrooms, spinach and passata. Sprinkle with cheddar cheese and nutmeg.

6 Continue layering the ingredients, seasoning well between the layers and finishing with a layer of lasagne topped with passata and cheese. Sprinkle with the remaining nutmeg and scatter the Parmesan over the top.

7 Bake in the oven for about 35–40 minutes, until a rich golden brown. Leave to stand for 10 minutes before cutting into squares to serve.

Marlon's tip
Being an international playboy traveller, I recommend using fresh porcini mushrooms. Many supermarkets sell them fresh or in packs of dried ones, but if you can't find them, you could use chestnut mushrooms instead.

Kelly's Speedy Spaghetti

It's a good job newlywed Roy Glover likes spaghetti, because it's the only meal Kelly can make. She would approve of this speedy recipe, which is easier to make than Bolognese, and is ready in only 20 minutes with a little help from the store-cupboard.

Serves 2

15ml/1 tablespoon olive oil
1 small onion, sliced
1 garlic clove, crushed
200g/7oz turkey mince
220g can chopped tomatoes
with herbs
200g/7oz spaghetti
salt and freshly ground
black pepper
40g/1½oz chopped
walnuts
30ml/2 tablespoons grated
Parmesan cheese

1 Heat the oil and fry the onion and garlic over a high heat until golden. Stir in the turkey and cook until browned. Add the tomatoes and bring to the boil. Simmer, uncovered, stirring occasionally, for 15 minutes.

2 Meanwhile, cook the spaghetti in boiling, lightly salted water for 8 minutes or according to the directions on the packet. Drain well, then toss with the sauce and adjust the seasoning to taste.

3 Stir in the walnuts and sprinkle with Parmesan to serve.

Kelly's tip
I used to be a vegetarian and you can make a good meat-free version of this recipe by using Quorn instead of the turkey mince.

Emily was over the moon when Viv agreed to take her on full-time in the village shop. She's a great asset and makes a smashing cup of tea, although Viv's not too keen on her egg sandwiches!

Seared Duck Breasts with Hot Plum Sauce

This simple yet sophisticated dish is one of Zoe's favourites – rich, sweet and spicy, ideal for a romantic dinner for two. However, with her track record, what she really needs to accompany the meal is the perfect partner to share it with.

Serves 2

2 large duck breast fillets
15ml/1 tablespoon
   vegetable oil
1 garlic clove, crushed
5ml/1 teaspoon grated fresh
   ginger
125ml/4fl oz claret
30ml/2 tablespoons red
   plum jam
1 small orange
10ml/2 teaspoons raspberry
   vinegar
salt and freshly ground
   black pepper

Tip

A candlelit setting and a good bottle of claret or a well-matured Rioja helps fuel the flames of romance a little further.

1 Use a sharp knife to slash a diamond pattern in the skin of the duck. Heat half the oil in a ridged griddle pan or heavy frying pan and place the breasts skin side down in the pan.

2 Cook on a fairly high heat until the skin is a rich golden brown, spooning away excess fat as it gathers in the pan. Lower the heat to moderate and turn the breasts over. Cook for a further 8–10 minutes, or until golden brown but slightly pink inside.

3 Remove the duck and keep hot. Drain the fat from the pan and add the remaining oil. Stir in the garlic and ginger, then add the wine and plum jam. Pare a thin strip of rind from the orange and squeeze the juice, then add these to the pan.

4 Bring to the boil and simmer gently for 4–5 minutes until reduced and slightly syrupy. Add the vinegar with salt and pepper to taste.

5 Return the duck breasts to the pan and simmer for 2 minutes. Serve immediately, with noodles or garlic mash, and a mixed leaf salad.

Bernice's Hot Pot

This tasty hot pot could have landed Bernice in hot water! She wanted to look after Alan, who was recuperating from his heart attack, and asked Gavin to buy the vegetables. Lazy Gavin produced the produce, but neglected to mention he had stolen it from Seth's prize vegetable garden! With Seth's prize leeks and carrots in the pot it was no wonder Alan pronounced it a delicious dish. The crime, however, caused a scandal in the village. Outraged Betty was convinced a jealous competitor had deliberately sabotaged Seth's veggies and pestered Sergeant Angie Reynolds to step up the police investigation. Thankfully, Gavin came clean at the summer fair and all was forgiven.

Serves 4

400g/14oz lean, boneless
   lamb neck fillet or leg
15ml/1 tablespoon
   Worcestershire sauce
900g/2lb potatoes
15ml/1 tablespoon
   sunflower oil
salt and freshly ground
   black pepper
15ml/1 tablespoon chopped
   fresh thyme
2 medium onions, finely
   chopped
2 medium leeks, sliced
2 medium carrots, sliced
15ml/1 tablespoon chopped
   fresh marjoram
15ml/1 tablespoon soy
   sauce
250ml/9fl oz lamb or beef
   stock
100ml/3½fl oz red wine

1 Preheat the oven to 170°C/325°F/Gas Mark 3. Trim any excess fat from the meat and cut into 3cm/1¼in pieces. Toss with the Worcestershire sauce to coat evenly.

2 Peel the potatoes and cut into 5mm/¼in thick slices. Brush the inside of a large casserole with a little oil and arrange a layer of about half the potatoes in the base. Sprinkle with salt, pepper and thyme.

3 Layer the lamb, onions, leeks and carrots in the pot, sprinkling with salt, pepper, thyme and marjoram between layers. Finish with a layer of potatoes.

4 Pour over the soy sauce, stock and wine. Brush the potatoes with the remaining oil. Cover closely with a lid or foil and bake in the oven for about 1 hour 30 minutes, then remove the lid and cook for a further 30 minutes to brown the potatoes.

Bernice's tip
Use a wide, heavy casserole dish for this, so the ingredients can be spread in a fairly shallow layer – this way, they cook evenly and the juices simmer down to a rich, dark gravy. Get a big strong man to carry it for you if you can.

Dingle Stew – Pork, Leek and Cider Casserole

One of Lisa Dingle's easy, economical standbys, this tasty stew is a classic combination of flavours, ideal for a family meal and good enough to impress Mrs Kirk, Paddy's snobby mother. Using both home-reared pork and home-grown vegetables means Lisa can afford to add the cider. It's simmered long and slow, so all the alcohol from the cider evaporates off during cooking leaving just the rich flavour behind.

Serves 4

500g/1lb 2oz shoulder or
    spare-rib pork
300g/10½oz leeks
15ml/1 tablespoon
    sunflower oil
2 crisp eating apples
300ml/½ pint strong dry
    cider
1 sprig of rosemary
salt and freshly ground
    black pepper
45ml/3 tablespoons soured
    cream
chopped fresh parsley to
    serve

1 Trim any excess fat from the meat and cut into 3cm/1¼in dice. Trim and wash the leeks and cut into 1cm/½in thick slices.

2 Heat the oil in a heavy flameproof casserole or pan and fry the meat over a fairly high heat for 4–5 minutes, stirring, until golden brown.

3 Add the leeks and cook for a further 3–4 minutes, until lightly coloured. Peel, core and cut the apple into 1cm/½in chunks. Add to the pan with the cider, rosemary, salt and pepper.

4 Bring to the boil, then cover and simmer gently for about 40 minutes, until the pork is tender. Remove the rosemary sprig and stir in the soured cream. Sprinkle with chopped parsley and serve hot, with mashed or new potatoes.

Tip
Crème fraîche makes a good alternative to soured cream – but we can't even pronounce it!

Parties and Special Occasions

Winter means long, cold nights in the village, but it's also the season of bonfires and punch to warm cold hands and hearts. Christmas is always a time for families and togetherness in Emmerdale. The village looks so pretty when the Christmas lights are up and the Christmas fair is an annual event that involves everyone, young and old, and invariably requires Pollard to do his annual good deed and dress up as Father Christmas! The Woolpack is always at the centre of special occasions, and in 1998 Alan invited most of the village to enjoy their Christmas dinner with him in the pub. That year's Christmas, however, had rather a bitter-sweet flavour. There was joy at the Dingles as Lisa gave birth to baby Belle and Marlon was reconciled with the family (so this year he'll be doing the cooking). At the post office, however, Vic's death meant a tragic holiday season for the Windsors.

Christmas at the Sugdens is very much a family occasion. With so many of the older generation gone or overseas, the focus is now on the younger members of the dynasty, including Andy, the foster child who was taken in by Jack and Sarah after being abandoned by his father at Christmas 1997.

Birthdays are also special occasions that all the villagers can get involved in. Little Alice Bates and Joseph Tate both had their birthday parties in the diner in 1999 and Marlon and Betty enjoyed the opportunity to cater for kids. And for the really special functions you can always rely on Eric and Marlon to pull out all the stops – even when, as at Kim and Steve's wedding, they didn't even get paid! The

original caterers pulled out when Steve's cheque bounced, so Eric had to cover at short notice. Outraged at being fleeced, he broke into Steve's cottage and took some of his belongings as payment! Marlon was pleased to make the effort for Mandy's wedding, but a word of advice – don't let Kelly anywhere near the wedding-cake mixture, whatever you do!

Tex-Mex Meatballs with Creamy Tomato Dip

The diner's fun American theme makes it a very popular location for birthday parties and family celebrations – especially if Marlon's doing the cooking. Children of all ages love his easy-to-make little meatballs with a dip, and they're inexpensive, too. For teenagers you could add a dash of chilli sauce to the mix, but for the younger tots, keep it milder.

Serves 4–6

220g/7oz can red kidney
    beans
1 large onion, very finely
    chopped
1 garlic clove, crushed
600g/1lb 5oz lean minced
    beef
1 small egg, beaten
60ml/4 tablespoons fresh
    white breadcrumbs
15ml/1 tablespoon chopped
    fresh parsley
5ml/1 teaspoon paprika
salt and freshly ground
    black pepper
1 packet taco corn chips

DIP
200g/7oz fromage frais
100ml/3½fl oz tomato taco
    salsa
chopped fresh parsley to
    garnish

1 Drain the kidney beans thoroughly and mash with a fork. Stir in the onion, garlic, beef, egg, breadcrumbs, parsley, paprika and seasonings and mix thoroughly with your hands.

2 Shape the mixture into 36 small balls (children may like to help with this part). Heat the oil in a wide, heavy-based frying pan and fry the meatballs in batches over a moderate heat for 10–12 minutes, turning often, until golden brown and thoroughly cooked. Lift on to absorbent kitchen paper to drain.

3 For the dip, tip the fromage frais into a small bowl and lightly swirl in the taco salsa to give a marbled effect. Sprinkle with parsley.

4 Place the bowl of dip in the centre of a large platter and pile the meatballs and taco chips around it to serve.

Marlon's tip
If you can't get hold of taco salsa from your nearest supermarket, cheat! Stir a few tablespoons of tomato ketchup into the fromage frais instead.

Emmerdale Christmas Butter Fudge

This buttery-smooth fudge has a warm, Christmassy spice flavour and makes a great gift, packed into pretty boxes for friends. It will store in an airtight container for about a month, but it's very more-ish, so you may not get the chance to keep it that long!

Makes about 650g/1lb 7oz

500g/1lb 2oz granulated sugar
115g/4oz butter
30ml/2 tablespoons golden syrup
170g/6oz can evaporated milk
15ml/1 tablespoon cherry brandy or brandy
2.5ml/½ teaspoon ground cinnamon

Sarah's tip

If you don't have a thermometer, test the mixture instead by dropping a teaspoonful of the mixture into cold water; if you can roll it into a soft ball, it's ready. The mixture will be very hot, so take care.

1 Brush an 18cm/7in square, shallow cake tin with melted butter. Place the sugar, butter, golden syrup and evaporated milk in a heavy-based pan.

2 Place the pan over a low heat and stir constantly, without boiling, until the sugar has dissolved completely.

3 Once the sugar has dissolved, bring to the boil and boil rapidly, stirring occasionally to prevent sticking, until the mixture reaches 118°C/240°F on a sugar thermometer.

4 Remove the pan from the heat and stir in the cherry brandy and cinnamon. Beat hard with a wooden spoon until the mixture becomes thick and creamy with a slightly granular texture.

5 Tip the mixture quickly into the prepared tin and smooth the surface level. Cool until almost set, then mark into squares with a knife. When completely cold and set, cut into squares and store in an airtight container.

Sarah's Plum 'n' Figgy Christmas Pudding

This classic recipe has been handed down through the generations, and comes out every year for Christmas. It's best to make it several months in advance, to give the flavours time to fully mature. Sarah always makes two, so there's always one in reserve, and it will store for next year if it's not used.

If you think making two Christmas puddings, as Sarah suggests, is good organization, how about this? Marlon once made a Christmas cake for the entire village. He used Lisa's cement mixer to mix it, and baked the cake in an old tin bath! Surprisingly, it was pronounced delicious by Alan Turner of all people.

**Makes 2 puddings, each
   serving 8**

200g/7oz currants
175g/6oz seedless raisins
175g/6oz sultanas
175g/6oz ready-to-eat
   prunes, chopped
100g/3½oz ready-to-eat
   dried figs, chopped
50g/1¾oz cut mixed peel
300ml/½ pint stout
60ml/4 tablespoons dark
   rum
175g/6oz dark muscovado
   sugar
100g/3½oz self-raising
   flour
7.5ml/1½ teaspoons mixed
   spice
2.5ml/½ teaspoon grated
   nutmeg
175g/6oz shredded suet
100g/3½oz fresh white
   breadcrumbs
50g/1¾oz blanched,
   chopped almonds
1 medium carrot, grated
finely grated rind of 1
   orange
3 large eggs, beaten

1 Lightly grease two 1.2 litre/2 pint pudding basins. Place the currants, raisins, sultanas, prunes, figs and peel in a bowl and pour over the stout and rum. Stir to mix evenly, then cover the bowl with clingfilm and leave to soak for several hours or overnight.

2 Stir the sugar into the fruit, mixing well. Sift together the flour, mixed spice and nutmeg, then stir into the fruit mixture. Stir in the suet, breadcrumbs, almonds, grated carrot and orange rind. Finally, add the eggs, mixing thoroughly to make a soft dropping consistency.

3 Divide the mixture between the two pudding basins, smoothing the surface level. Cover with a double thickness of pleated greaseproof paper and foil. Tie with string to secure.

4 Steam or boil the puddings for 5 hours, topping up the water as necessary. Remove and cool completely. Cover with fresh paper and foil before storing in a cool, dry place for up to 2 years.

5 To serve, steam or boil the puddings for a further 2 hours, then turn out and serve with rum sauce or brandy butter.

Sarah's tip

Annie would have something to say about this, but if you have a microwave, save time and avoid a steamy kitchen on Christmas Day by reheating the pud in the microwave. Remove the foil and cook on High (100% power) for 8 minutes, then leave to stand for 3–4 minutes before serving.

Marlon's Festive Christmas Turkey

Marlon's Christmas dinners are spectacular – and he has had a lot of practice. One year he spent Christmas Day making two full dinners with all the trimmings, one for Pollard's wine bar and one for the Dingles family celebrations. Mind you, it didn't do him any good, because he was later cast out by the family – after they'd all stuffed their faces, of course!

Serves 6, plus enough to serve cold

50g/1¾oz butter
1 medium onion, chopped
1 garlic clove, crushed
1 crisp dessert apple
175g/6oz fresh white breadcrumbs
50g/1¾oz chopped walnuts
15ml/1 tablespoon dried sage
finely grated rind and juice of 1 large orange
5kg/11lb oven-ready turkey
salt and freshly ground black pepper
12 streaky bacon rashers
fresh orange slices and sage leaves to garnish

1 Preheat the oven to 190°C/375°F/Gas Mark 5. Melt half the butter and fry the onion and garlic for 3–4 minutes to soften.

2 Core and coarsely grate the apple and add to the breadcrumbs with the onion, garlic, walnuts, sage, orange rind and juice. Use the mixture to stuff the neck end of the turkey. Mould any spare stuffing into small balls and place on a baking sheet.

3 Place the turkey in a roasting tin, spread the remaining butter over the breast and sprinkle with salt and pepper. Cover loosely with foil and roast in the oven for 3–3¼ hours, until there is no trace of pink in the juices. Remove the foil for the final hour to brown and crisp the breast.

4 Cut the bacon rashers in half crossways, then roll up firmly. Place on the baking sheet with the stuffing balls. Cook in the oven on the shelf above the turkey for the final 20–25 minutes cooking time, until golden brown.

5 When the turkey is cooked, lift it on to a serving plate and surround with the bacon rolls and stuffing balls. Garnish with orange slices and sprigs of sage.

Marlon's tip

You don't want to get on the wrong side of relatives like my Uncle Zak, so plan this carefully. It's a good idea to time the turkey so it's cooked about 20 minutes ahead of serving, then cover it loosely with foil and allow to stand in a warm place for about 20 minutes before carving. This makes it much easier to carve so you won't be running round like a headless chicken.

The Dingles always look forward to Christmas dinner. There's always enough for second helpings – and third, and fourth!

Seth and Betty made a swinging impression as Fred and Ginger at the Hollywood theme night.

Betty's Special Pumpkin Soup

Seth was once caught cheating in a village competition for the heaviest pumpkin – he'd filled his full of shot and nails. Thankfully, things have improved a little since then. Betty now asks him to keep back one of his best prize pumpkins for this recipe, so it can be hollowed out and used as an impressive container to serve the soup in, once the flesh has been scooped out.

Serves 8

30ml/2 tablespoons
   sunflower oil
2 medium onions, chopped
200g/7oz carrots, chopped
5ml/1 teaspoon ground
   allspice
600g/1lb 5oz pumpkin flesh,
   chopped
400g/14oz can plum
   tomatoes
1.5 litres/2¾ pints chicken or
   vegetable stock
100g/3½oz split orange
   lentils
juice of 1 lemon
salt and pepper
freshly grated nutmeg and
   chopped fresh parsley to
   serve

1 Heat the oil in a large pan and fry the onions and carrots over a moderate heat for 3–4 minutes, stirring occasionally, until softened. Stir in the allspice.

2 Add the pumpkin, tomatoes, stock and lentils and stir until boiling. Reduce the heat to a simmer, then cover the pan and simmer gently for about 30 minutes, or until the ingredients are softened.

3 Remove from the heat and purée the soup in a blender or food processor until smooth. Return to the pan and add the lemon juice, then adjust the seasoning to taste with salt and pepper.

4 Reheat until boiling, then serve sprinkled with nutmeg and parsley.

Betty's tip
The wind in the Dales can really chill your bones, so for an extra warming soup, replace the allspice with a teaspoonful of Madras curry spice.

Salmon en Croûte

Eric will always find a dish to impress on a grand occasion, if only to outdo everyone else's efforts! He provided the catering for Kim and Steve's wedding, and this is his suggestion for Mandy and Paddy's wedding. It certainly looks impressive, and although Eric wouldn't admit it, it's really not as difficult as it looks. Ask your fishmonger to fillet the salmon and remove the skin for you.

Eric wonders how he can convince Stella to invest in a health and beauty spa, so he can charge her extra for some second-hand fitness equipment.

Serves 8

PASTRY
400g/14oz plain flour
2.5ml/½ teaspoon salt
200g/7oz butter
1 small egg
cold water to mix
beaten egg to glaze

FILLING
200g/7oz frozen leaf
    spinach, thawed
75g/2¾oz butter
15ml/1 tablespoon lemon
    juice
10ml/2 teaspoons grated
    fresh ginger
2.5ml/½ teaspoon grated
    nutmeg
salt and freshly ground
    black pepper
2kg/4lb 8oz whole salmon,
    filleted and skinned
175g/6oz peeled cooked
    prawns

1 Sift the flour and salt and rub in the butter with your finger-tips until the mixture resembles breadcrumbs. Beat the egg with 45ml/3 tablespoons cold water and stir into the mixture to bind the dough together, adding more cold water as necessary to make a soft but not sticky dough. Cover and chill for 20 minutes.

2 Preheat the oven to 200°C/400°F/Gas Mark 6. Press as much moisture as possible from the spinach. Beat the butter to soften, then mix with the lemon juice, ginger, nutmeg, salt and pepper.

3 Roll out half the pastry to a rectangle a little larger than one salmon fillet and place on a baking sheet. Place a salmon fillet on top, skin side down, and spread with the ginger butter. Arrange the prawns and spinach leaves over this, then top with the remaining salmon fillet, skin side up.

4 Roll out the remaining pastry to cover the salmon, moisten the edge of the pastry base with beaten egg and press the covering pastry down firmly to seal.

5 Roll out the pastry trimmings and stamp out small rounds with a 2cm/¾ in cutter. Brush the covered salmon with egg and arrange the pastry 'scales' over it. Cut a tail and eyes from the remaining pastry and fix in place, then glaze the whole salmon with beaten egg.

6 Bake in the oven for 35–40 minutes, or until the pastry is firm and golden brown. Serve warm or cold, with salad.

Eric's tip
If you want to prepare the salmon in pastry in advance, you can shape it ready for the oven, then cover it with clingfilm and store it in the refrigerator for up to 24 hours, ready for baking on the big day. The pastry will brown more evenly if you turn the baking sheet around in the oven about halfway through the cooking time.

Yorkshire Parkin Pigs

Little Joseph Tate and Victoria-Anne Sugden can't resist these piggy gingerbread parkin biscuits, which are handed out around the bonfire on November the Fifth. They are traditionally cut with a pig-shaped cutter, but if you don't have one, they could be cut with a gingerbread-man cutter instead.

Makes about 12

225g/8oz plain flour
10ml/2 teaspoons ground
    ginger
5ml/1 teaspoon bicarbonate
    of soda
50g/1¾oz medium oatmeal
60ml/4 tablespoons golden
    syrup
50g/1¾oz dark brown
    muscovado sugar
75g/2¾oz butter
1 medium egg, beaten
currants for decoration

1 Preheat the oven to 180°C/350°F/Gas Mark 4. Sift the flour, ginger and bicarbonate of soda into a bowl and stir in the oatmeal. Make a well in the centre.

2 Place the syrup, sugar and butter in a pan and heat gently, stirring, until melted. Remove from the heat and pour into the flour. Add the egg and stir to mix well.

3 Mix to a fairly soft dough, then cool slightly. Turn out on to a lightly floured surface and roll out to about 5mm/¼in thick. Cut out about 12 pig shapes.

4 Lift on to a lightly greased baking sheet. Press currants into the biscuits to resemble eyes, then bake for 15–20 minutes or until firm and golden brown.

5 Cool for a few minutes on the baking sheets then lift carefully on to a wire rack to cool. Store in an airtight container for up to a week.

Tip

If the dough is too soft and sticky to manage, wrap it in clingfilm and place in the fridge for 10–15 minutes to allow it to firm slightly before rolling.

Pink Champagne Sorbet with Lemon Hearts

Mandy and Paddy chose this sweet dish for their wedding reception. They might have got to try it too, if only Hotten Constabulary provided room service! It helps if you have an electric ice-cream maker for this recipe, as it makes a very smooth-textured ice very easily, but it's by no means essential, as whisking will give a very good result, too.

Serves 6–8

**1 bottle rosé champagne or
    sparkling wine**
40g/1½oz icing sugar

HEARTS
175g/6oz plain flour
115g/4oz butter
80g/3oz golden caster sugar
**finely grated zest of 1
    lemon**
1 egg yolk
15ml/1 tablespoon milk
icing sugar to sprinkle

1 Mix a little of the champagne with the icing sugar, stirring to dissolve it thoroughly.

2 If you have an ice-cream maker, freeze the mixture in this according to the manufacturer's instructions. Alternatively, pour into a large freezer-proof container and freeze for 3–4 hours, whisking hard at hourly intervals to break up the ice crystals.

3 Meanwhile, to make the hearts, sift the flour into a bowl and rub in the butter evenly with your fingertips. Stir in the sugar and lemon zest. Mix the egg yolk and milk, then stir into the mix, kneading lightly to a firm dough. Wrap the dough in clingfilm and chill for 30 minutes.

4 Preheat the oven to 190°C/375°F/Gas Mark 5. Roll out thinly on a lightly floured surface and cut 18–20 biscuits with a heart-shaped cutter. Place on a baking sheet and bake for about 15 minutes or until firm and golden brown. Cool on a wire rack and sprinkle with icing sugar.

5 Serve the sorbet in small scoops arranged in stemmed glasses, with the lemon heart biscuits on the side.

Mandy's tip
There's more important things to think about on your wedding day than biscuits. Make them in advance and store in an airtight container in the freezer for up to 1 month. Thaw at room temperature.

Nutty Sandwich Men

Perfect for a children's birthday party, kids will love these simple sandwiches, and the fillings can be varied to suit all ages and tastes. Kathy uses different shapes to match party themes.

Makes 8

1 ripe banana
100g/3½oz smooth peanut
    butter
100g/3½oz low-fat soft
    cheese
1 small punnet of mustard
    and cress
30ml/2 tablespoons
    chopped dates or sultanas
8 large thin slices of white
    bread
8 large thin slices of brown
    bread

1 To make the two fillings, chop the banana and mix with the peanut butter. Mix together the soft cheese, mustard and cress and sultanas.

2 Spread 4 slices of white bread with the peanut butter filling, then top each with a slice of brown bread, pressing down firmly.

3 Spread 4 slices of white bread with the cream cheese filling and top each with a slice of brown bread, pressing down firmly.

4 Using a gingerbread man cutter, cut the sandwiches into shapes. Arrange the sandwich men, some white side up, some brown side up, on a platter, and cover with clingfilm until needed.

Kathy's tip
These two fillings are both healthy choices for children, but avoid using the peanut butter if any children have a nut allergy, and stick instead with the cream cheese filling or choose another variation of your own.

Right: In this charming ensemble it's hardly surprising that Reg Holdsworth mistook Butch for a successful retailing entrepreneur!

Marlon's Croquembouche Tower

Not to be outdone by Eric, Marlon shows his pâtisserie skills with this classic French-style pastry wedding creation for Mandy and Paddy. It's a tall pyramid of choux puffs, glazed with spun caramel.

Serves about 12

PUFFS
100g/3½oz butter
300ml/½ pint water
125g/4½oz plain flour
4 medium eggs, beaten

FILLING
300ml/½ pint double cream
300ml/½ pint whipping
  cream
5ml/1 teaspoon vanilla
  essence
30ml/2 tablespoons icing
  sugar

TO DECORATE
200g/7oz caster sugar
100ml/3½fl oz water
crystallized rose petals

Marlon's tip
Take care when handling the caramel as it is dangerously hot – unless Eric Pollard's in the vicinity. If you're not confident about spinning the caramel in fine threads, drizzle it lightly over the buns instead.

1 Place the butter and water in a saucepan and heat until boiling. Remove from the heat and quickly tip in all the flour at once, beating with an electric whisk.

2 Return to a gentle heat and continue beating until the mixture begins to come away from the sides of the pan cleanly. Remove from the heat and cool slightly. Beat in the eggs gradually, until the mixture is smooth and shiny. Cool and chill.

3 Preheat the oven to 220°C/425°F/Gas Mark 7. Spoon the dough into a large piping bag fitted with a 1cm/½in plain nozzle. Pipe 50 walnut-sized balls on to wet baking sheets. Bake for 15–20 minutes until well-risen and golden brown.

4 Cut a slit in each puff with a sharp knife to release the steam and return to the oven for 4–5 minutes to dry out. Cool on a wire rack.

5 For the filling, whip the creams, vanilla and sugar together until the mixture is thick enough to just hold its shape. Spoon into a large piping bag and pipe into the buns.

6 Place the sugar and water in a heavy-based pan and heat gently without boiling until dissolved. Bring to the boil and boil rapidly to 138°C/280°F on a thermometer. Remove from the heat and dip the base of the pan in cold water.

7 Working quickly, dip the base of each puff into the caramel and pile up into a pyramid on a platter. Using 2 forks, throw fine strands of the caramel over the pyramid. Scatter with crystallized rose petals.

Lambs' Wool Punch

This classic hot spiced drink is a traditional old English wassail punch, served at Christmas-time for special celebrations in the Woolpack, and is always served to the carol-singers. Cider is used in many other parts of England, but it's more usual to use a good strong Yorkshire ale in Emmerdale.

Serves 10

4 crisp dessert apples, such
   as Cox's Orange Pippin
20 whole cloves
1 litre/1¾ pints brown ale
2 cinnamon sticks
5ml/1 teaspoon grated
   nutmeg
5ml/1 teaspoon ground
   ginger
500ml/18fl oz sweet white
   wine
125g/4½oz light muscovado
   sugar

Alan's tip
As a licensed victualler of many years' experience, I advise you not to boil the punch, so keep the heat low, or the alcohol will evaporate and you'll spoil the flavour.

1 Preheat the oven to 180°C/350°F/Gas Mark 4. Wash and dry the apples and stud with cloves. Place in an ovenproof dish with 45ml/3 tablespoons of the ale. Cover and bake for 20–25 minutes or until tender.

2 Put the remaining ale in a large pan with the remaining spices and bring slowly to a simmer. Add the wine and enough sugar to sweeten to taste. Keep the heat low and leave the punch without boiling for about 5 minutes to infuse the flavours.

3 Place the baked apples in a large punchbowl or heatproof bowl and strain the punch over them. It will froth up, hence the name 'lambs' wool'! Ladle into heatproof glasses or mugs to serve.

Cheeseburger Birthday Cake

Kathy makes this simple cake for children's parties at the diner. Made with just a simple all-in-one sponge and bought ready-to-roll icing, it's really very easy, yet looks very effective.

Serves 8–10

SPONGE CAKE
2 medium eggs
115g/4oz soft (tub) margarine
115g/4oz caster sugar
115g/4oz self-raising flour
5ml/1 teaspoon baking powder
finely grated rind of 1 lemon

TO DECORATE
apricot jam
250g/9oz ready-to-roll white icing
brown food colouring
115g/4oz thick chocolate spread
30ml/2 tablespoons chocolate hundreds and thousands
75g/2¾oz green ready-to-roll icing
75g/2¾oz yellow ready-to-roll icing
sesame seeds

1 Preheat the oven to 170°C/325°F/Gas Mark 3. Grease and base-line two 18cm/7in round sandwich tins.

2 Place all the ingredients for the cake in a large bowl and beat well until smooth and evenly mixed. Divide between the tins and smooth the top. Bake in the oven for 20–25 minutes, or until firm and golden brown. Turn out and cool on a wire rack.

3 Warm the jam and brush over the cakes. Knead a little brown colouring into the white icing to make a pale golden colour. Roll out and use to cover the cakes, smoothing evenly. (This will give the effect of a bun.)

4 Roll the green icing out and crimp the edges slightly to resemble lettuce leaves. Arrange over one cake, with crimped edges outwards.

5 Spoon the chocolate spread into an icing bag with a large plain nozzle, and pipe in the centre of the cake to resemble a large burger. Sprinkle the edges with chocolate hundreds and thousands.

6 Roll out the yellow icing, cut into 4 triangles and place over the 'burger', so the points stick out like a slice of cheese. Place the remaining cake on top and sprinkle the top with sesame seeds.

 Kathy's tip
If you don't have a piping bag, don't worry, just spread the chocolate spread as evenly as possible to make the burger shape.

Barbecues and Picnics

The glorious Dales countryside allows plenty of opportunity for dining alfresco in the summertime. Traditionally, barbecues at Home Farm and the Woolpack are events for the whole village to enjoy, while picnics have always been a great way for couples and families to spend time alone and enjoy the country air with a good spread. These recipes are designed with that in mind.

Thankfully, fast food hasn't hit Emmerdale yet. There are no chippies or kebab shops – one experience with Mandy's Munchbox was more than enough for most! Mandy's original plan was to convert an abandoned old caravan, replete with red drapes, leopardskin and a naked Dave Glover, into Mandy's Mobile Nookie Nest, but she eventually decided it was better to use the cooking skills she'd picked up in prison for financial reward. Several of the recipes in this chapter take their inspiration from Mandy's entrepreneurial spirit, if not

her standards of food hygiene. The environmental health inspector discovered a mousetrap in the Munchbox and Mandy picking a burger up off the floor ready to serve! The Munchbox was eventually blown up by a rival burger gang but these dishes are perfectly safe as long as you follow the instructions.

The Sugden family have farmed in Emmerdale since the 1850s.

The double porky burgers are also a Dingle favourite – they choose which one of their own pigs best suits the recipe! They have also been known to make their own beefburgers, after Roy Glover ran over one of the Sugdens' cows in his sister's Mini. Zak took the carcass home and made his own mince! The Down Under Dingle influence can also be seen in a couple of these outdoor dining ideas, gleaned from the time when the Woolpackers went on their first – and only – international tour.

There are also a couple of dishes that add a new twist to staple Dales/picnic food – lamb kebabs and chicken avocado wraps. These show the Woolpack bar menu's wide-ranging influences under Bernice – she's sure Alan will approve or make his feelings known if he doesn't. Alan himself contributes his special Scotch eggs, perfect for quick low-fat picnic snacks.

Lamb Kofta Kebabs with Minted Apricot Salsa

Fresh lamb is a staple in Dales kitchens, and this recipe adds a new twist to an old favourite. These Middle Eastern-style skewers with a delectable fruit salsa made their appearance on the Woolpack menu when Marlon took over in the kitchen. They can be made in advance and stored in the fridge, and take only minutes to cook on a barbecue or grill. They are also just as good served cold, for picnics.

Kathy and Marlon celebrated writing up the new menu for the diner.

Serves 4

550g/1lb 4oz lean, finely
minced lamb
25g/1oz fresh white
breadcrumbs
1 garlic clove, crushed
1 medium onion, grated
5ml/1 teaspoon ground
coriander
5ml/1 teaspoon ground
cumin
30ml/2 tablespoons
chopped fresh mint
salt and freshly ground
black pepper
olive oil for brushing

SALSA
200g/7oz fresh apricots (or
canned, drained apricots)
½ a small red onion
5ml/1 teaspoon grated
fresh ginger
juice of ½ a lime
30ml/2 tablespoons
chopped fresh mint
15ml/1 tablespoon extra
virgin olive oil
dash of Tabasco sauce
salt and freshly ground
black pepper

1 Using your hands, thoroughly mix together the lamb, breadcrumbs, garlic, onion, coriander, cumin, mint, salt and pepper.

2 Divide the mixture into 8 equal portions and use your hands to shape around 8 bamboo or metal skewers. Brush with olive oil.

3 To make the salsa, halve, stone and finely dice the apricots. Peel and grate the onion. Toss together the apricots, onion, ginger, lime juice, mint, oil and Tabasco, then season to taste with salt and pepper.

4 Cook the kofta kebabs on a moderately hot barbecue or grill for 10–12 minutes, turning occasionally, until golden brown and thoroughly cooked. Serve with the apricot salsa and couscous.

Marlon's tip
It helps if the lamb for this recipe is finely minced, so that the koftas have a really smooth texture. If it is too coarse, pop it in the food processor and pulse for a few seconds to chop it a little finer. If you use bamboo skewers, soak them in water for about 15 minutes before use, to prevent them burning on the barbecue or grill.

Venison Steaks in Guinness Marinade

Besides Betty, there are two things Seth loves most – living off the land and enjoying a tipple. This recipe combines them both, using one of Seth's favourite ways of cooking venison – soaked in a rich, spiced citrus marinade, with grilled red onions served alongside.

Serves 4

4 venison steaks
4 small red onions, halved
6 juniper berries
1 cinnamon stick
2 bay leaves
**finely grated zest and juice
of 1 orange**
200ml/7fl oz Guinness

1 Arrange the venison steaks and onions in a wide, shallow, non-metallic dish. Lightly crush the juniper and cinnamon, then add to the dish with the bay leaves, orange zest and juice.

2 Pour over the Guinness, then turn the meat to coat evenly. Cover and leave to marinade in the refrigerator for about 2 hours or overnight.

3 Drain the meat and onions, reserving the marinade, then cook both on a hot barbecue or grill for about 8–10 minutes, turning once and brushing occasionally with the reserved marinade. The cooking time of the meat will vary depending on thickness.

4 Serve the venison with the onions, crusty bread and salad.

Seth's tip
Some folks like their venison done slightly pink inside, but if you've a mind to, cook it for a little longer and serve it well done instead. And don't show Betty the recipe or she'll wonder where the rest of the Guinness got to.

Fruit Kebabs with Marshmallow Fondue

These luscious kebabs are one of Victoria's favourites, and they're a good way to encourage children of any age to eat more fruit. Young ones can help to thread the fruit on to the skewers, but make sure an adult is around when they're cooking.

Serves 4

2 bananas
2 kiwifruit
1 crisp eating apple
12 strawberries
15g/½oz butter
juice of ½ a lemon
2.5ml/½ teaspoon ground
   cinnamon

FONDUE
16 marshmallows
100ml/3½fl oz single cream
100g/3½oz plain chocolate
   dots
5ml/1 teaspoon vanilla
   essence

1 Peel the bananas and cut into thick chunks. Peel the kiwifruit and cut into quarters. Core the apple and cut into 8 chunks. Remove the tops from the strawberries. Thread the fruit pieces on to 8 bamboo skewers.

2 Melt the butter and add the lemon juice and cinnamon. Brush over the fruit on the skewers.

3 For the fondue, place all the ingredients in a small pan and heat gently without boiling, stirring, over a low heat until just melted. Remove from the heat.

4 Cook the kebabs on a hot barbecue or grill for 4–5 minutes, turning occasionally, until lightly browned. Serve with the marshmallow fondue for dipping, or spoon it over the kebabs just before serving.

 Sarah's tip
I try to get the children to try all kinds of fruit so this recipe can be varied depending on what's available, or on your own taste – try chunks of pineapple, mango, peaches or pears.

Chicken Avocado Tortilla Wraps with Lime Mayonnaise

The Dingle clan spreads far and wide, but as far as Marlon knows they have no Mexican connections. That doesn't stop him creating this tortilla wrap. This is a popular lunchtime special on the Woolpack bar menu, and it's also a good recipe to use for picnics. The soft tortilla wraps keep the tasty chicken filling firmly in place during transit.

Serves 4

60ml/4 tablespoons mayonnaise
15ml/1 tablespoon fromage frais or natural yogurt
finely grated zest and juice of 1 lime
4 soft flour tortillas
1 small red onion, thinly sliced
30ml/2 tablespoons chopped fresh coriander
2 small ripe avocados
400g/14oz cooked chicken (or 4 cooked chicken breasts)
salt and freshly ground black pepper

1 Mix together the mayonnaise, fromage frais and lime zest. Lay the tortillas out flat on a work surface and spread the mayonnaise over the centre of each.

2 Arrange the onion slices over the mayonnaise, then sprinkle with coriander.

3 Halve the avocados and remove the stone, then scoop out the flesh with a large spoon. Slice the flesh and sprinkle with lime juice. Slice the chicken and sprinkle with lime juice.

4 Divide the chicken and avocado mixture between the tortillas and sprinkle with salt and pepper. Wrap the tortillas firmly around the filling and either eat immediately or pack into boxes to take on your picnic.

 Marlon's tip
Tortillas often come in a large pack containing several – if you want to keep the rest, seal the pack and they will keep in the fridge for a couple of days, or in the freezer for about a month. Thaw at room temperature.

Chilli Beanburgers

Both vegetarians and meat-eaters can enjoy these healthy, low-fat veggie burgers from the diner. Serve them in a sesame bun or just as they are with a fresh mixed salad.

Serves 4

15ml/1 tablespoon olive oil
1 small onion, finely
   chopped
1 garlic clove, crushed
5ml/1 teaspoon ground
   cumin
5ml/1 teaspoon ground
   coriander
1.25ml/¼ teaspoon crushed
   dried chillies
100g/3½oz mushrooms,
   finely chopped
400g/14oz can red kidney
   beans, drained
50g/1¾oz fresh white
   breadcrumbs
30ml/2 tablespoons chopped
   fresh coriander
salt and freshly ground
   black pepper
flour for shaping
olive oil to brush

1 Heat the oil in a large pan and fry the onion and garlic, stirring over a moderate heat for 2–3 minutes or until softened. Add the cumin, coriander and chillies and cook for about 30 seconds, stirring.

2 Add the mushrooms and cook, stirring, until all of the moisture has evaporated. Remove from the heat.

3 Mash the beans with a fork and add to the pan with the breadcrumbs. Stir in the fresh coriander, mixing thoroughly. Season well with salt and pepper.

4 Using lightly floured hands, shape the mixture into 4 flat burger shapes.

5 Brush the burgers with oil and cook on a hot barbecue for about 8–10 minutes, turning once, until golden brown. Serve with a spoonful of Greek-style yogurt or relish.

Kathy's tip
These burgers will freeze well for up to a month – just shape them as usual and pack in an airtight container with leaves of non-stick paper between. If you plan to store them for longer than a month, omit the garlic.

The environmental health inspector wonders if mouseburgers are today's special Munchbox offer.

Mandy's Double Porky Burgers

These mildly spiced burgers from Mandy's Munchbox venture have a surprise inside – use your favourite chutney or pickle. They're great for barbecues, but you could cook them under an ordinary grill instead if it rains.

Serves 4

15ml/1 tablespoon
   sunflower oil
1 garlic clove, crushed
1 small onion, finely
   chopped
500g/1lb 2oz lean minced
   pork
40g/1½oz fresh brown or
   white breadcrumbs
5ml/1 teaspoon dried sage
salt and freshly ground
   black pepper
20ml/4 teaspoons chutney
   or mixed pickle

1 Heat the oil and fry the garlic and onion gently for about 3–4 minutes, to soften.

2 Mix together the pork, breadcrumbs and sage, then mix in the onions and season well with salt and pepper.

3 Shape the mixture into 8 round burgers, and place a spoonful of chutney in the middle of 4 of them. Top each with another round and press the edges to seal in the pickle, shaping to thick burger shapes.

4 Cook the burgers on a hot barbecue or grill for about 10 minutes, turning once, until golden brown and thoroughly cooked. Serve in toasted burger buns with salad.

Oz-style 'Alligator' Steaks with Marlon's Special Relish

No, not really alligator – they're actually turkey steaks. When the Dingles returned from Oz with tales of throwing alligator and roo steaks on the barbie, Marlon got carried away and was inspired to create his own version.

Serves 4

1 garlic clove, crushed
15ml/1 tablespoon soy
   sauce
15ml/1 tablespoon lime
   juice
10ml/2 teaspoons clear
   honey
5ml/1 teaspoon sesame oil
5ml/1 teaspoon paprika
1.25ml/¼ teaspoon
   cayenne pepper
4 turkey breast steaks

MARLON'S RELISH
1 medium, ripe mango
1 ripe kiwifruit
1 small fresh red chilli
2 spring onions
finely grated rind and juice
   of ½ a lime
45ml/3 tablespoons
   chopped coriander
garlic salt and freshly
   ground black pepper

1 Mix together the garlic, soy, lime juice, honey, oil, paprika and cayenne in a wide dish, then add the turkey steaks and turn to coat evenly. Cover and chill to marinate for about 30 minutes.

2 Meanwhile, to make the relish, peel, stone and finely dice the mango. Peel and finely dice the kiwifruit. De-seed and finely chop the chilli. Trim and finely slice the spring onions.

3 Mix together the mango, kiwifruit, chilli and spring onions and add the lime rind, juice and coriander. Stir to mix well, then add garlic salt and pepper to taste.

4 Cook the steaks on a moderately hot barbecue for 8–10 minutes, turning once, until thoroughly cooked. Serve hot, with the relish spooned over.

Alan's Special Scotch Eggs

The thing that makes this recipe special is that it is much lower in fat than traditional Scotch eggs – so Alan Turner can keep to a healthy diet even when enjoying a summer picnic. Served with a fresh tomato salad, they're a real treat, whether you're watching your diet or not.

Serves 4

1 hard-boiled egg
115g/4oz skimmed-milk soft cheese
45ml/3 tablespoons chopped fresh chives
500g/1lb 2oz half-fat sausagemeat
salt and freshly ground black pepper
30ml/2 tablespoons skimmed milk
75g/2¾oz porridge oats

1 Preheat the oven to 200°C/400°F/Gas Mark 6. Peel and finely chop the hard-boiled egg and mix with the cheese and chives. Season with salt and pepper. Shape into 4 small balls.

2 Divide the sausagemeat into 4 equal pieces and use floured hands to press each to a flat round shape. Place a cheese ball in the centre of each and draw the edges of the sausagemeat up around it to enclose, smoothing over the join to seal completely.

3 Brush each 'egg' with milk and roll in the porridge oats to coat evenly. Place on a baking sheet and bake in the oven for 30–35 minutes or until golden brown. Serve warm or cold, with salad.

Alan's tip

I get half-fat sausagemeat from the Woolpack's suppliers, but if you can't find it, look out for half-fat sausages instead. Then simply slit the skins and remove the meat inside. Or you can make a vegetarian version using vegetarian sausage mix.

Betty's Crunchy Cabbage and Apple Slaw

Betty knows that one of the many benefits of living with Seth is a guaranteed supply of fresh vegetables. She takes the pick of his best cabbage, celery and carrots for this colourful, healthy salad which stays crisp for hours, with a light herb dressing to bring out the flavours. It's the ideal accompaniment for barbecued meats and fish, or with cold sliced meats and cheese for picnics.

Serves 4

150g/5½oz white cabbage
1 celery stick
150g/5½oz carrots
1 crisp red eating apple
15ml/1 tablespoon lime juice
2 spring onions
100ml/3½fl oz mayonnaise
45ml/3 tablespoons low-fat
    natural yogurt
15ml/1 tablespoon chopped
    fresh chervil or parsley
15ml/1 tablespoon chopped
    fresh mint
salt and freshly ground
    black pepper
paprika to sprinkle

1 Trim and finely shred the cabbage and celery. Peel and coarsely grate the carrots, core and grate the apple and toss in the lime juice. Finely chop the spring onions.

2 Mix together the mayonnaise, yogurt, chervil and mint, then taste and adjust the seasoning with salt and pepper.

3 Mix together all the prepared ingredients, pour over the dressing and toss thoroughly to coat evenly. Sprinkle with paprika and serve cold.

Betty's tip

If your fingers aren't as nimble as they used to be, use a food processor – the preparation time is greatly reduced. Choose a fine shredding blade for the cabbage and celery, and a medium grating blade for the carrots and apple.

Down-under Picnic Salad

A clever idea with Aussie influences, with the sort of flavour combinations typical of modern Australia – something the Dingles may well have tried out on their visit there. The salad is made in layers, but upside-down, complete with dressing, so the dressing won't coat the ingredients until the bowl is inverted, thus avoiding any soggy lettuce when you reach your destination.

Serves 4

DRESSING
5ml/1 teaspoon grated
    fresh ginger
5ml/1 teaspoon wholegrain
    mustard
2.5ml/½ teaspoon Australian
    honey
15ml/1 tablespoon
    raspberry vinegar
75ml/5 tablespoons olive oil
salt and freshly ground
    black pepper

SALAD
1 firm, ripe avocado
15ml/1 tablespoon lime
    juice
2 smoked streaky bacon
    rashers
100g/3½oz beansprouts
2 medium tomatoes
½ a Cos lettuce

1 Make the dressing by placing all the ingredients in a screw-topped jar and shaking well to mix evenly. Pour into the base of a deep picnic container or mixing bowl.

2 Halve the avocado, peel and remove the stone. Cut into dice, then toss in lime juice to coat evenly. Place in the bowl.

3 Dice the bacon and fry in its own fat until golden and crisp. Drain and cool, then scatter over the avocado. Top with a layer of beansprouts. Slice the tomatoes and arrange over the beansprouts. Shred the lettuce and arrange over the top.

4 Cover with a lid or clingfilm, then, when ready to serve, turn out the salad into a bowl to let the dressing run through the ingredients.

Butch's tip
If you find it difficult to buy fresh beansprouts, why not grow your own? Emily grows her own beansprouts and it's dead easy to do. She got some dried mung beans from a health food shop. What you do next is soak them in cold water overnight, then place on dampened kitchen paper in a large jar; rinse in cold water every day, and you'll have fresh sprouted beans in just 3–4 days. Brilliant.

Mandy's Munchbox Big Picnic Loaf

What with cooking for the Dingle family and running her Munchbox catering business, Mandy has had plenty of experience of catering for large appetites. This giant sandwich is easy to transport on a picnic, and is enough to feed a whole crowd!

Serves 4–6

1 French baguette
1 garlic clove
30ml/2 tablespoons olive oil
30ml/2 tablespoons
    creamed horseradish
4 beef tomatoes, sliced
salt and freshly ground
    black pepper
8 thin slices salami or
    smoked ham
1 green pepper, thinly sliced
6 small gherkins, sliced

1 Slice the baguette in half lengthwise. Cut the garlic clove in half and rub it over the cut surface of the bread. Drizzle the olive oil over the cut side of the bottom half of the loaf. Spread the horseradish over the top half.

2 Arrange the tomato slices over the bottom half of the bread and sprinkle with salt and pepper. Top with the salami or ham, then the pepper and gherkins.

3 Place the top half of the bread over the filling and press down firmly. Wrap the whole loaf fairly tightly in foil to take on your picnic. Cut into thick chunks to serve when you reach your destination.

Mandy's tip
Don't forget to pack a sharp knife to take with you on your picnic to cut the loaf. You can't scoff it all in one go.

Opposite: Mandy once poisoned a group of quarry-site protestors with her special vegeburgers. She had followed a recipe that she found in Hotten Library, and was very proud that the vegetable oil she used was 'low in polyunsaturates'. However, she had failed to cook the kidney beans properly, and the end result made everyone sick!

Puddings and Desserts

S arah still finds being a farmer's wife very hard to cope with at times, and the Sugdens' ongoing financial problems have only exacerbated her frustrations in recent months. She took a part-time job at the diner to help pay the bills and, although it didn't meet with Jack's approval, it has allowed her to use one of the most valuable skills she picked up on the farm. When she first moved to Emmerdale Sarah's cooking was the joke of the family, but luckily Annie was a superb teacher. Sarah was determined to succeed against the odds – one year she made cake after cake to try and compete with Annie for the Hotten Show's Best Cake competition. Annie had always won, but that particular year Sarah's persistence paid off and she was awarded first prize! When Annie decided to retire to Spain, she handed over control of the kitchen to Sarah, who has coped admirably since with the running of the farm, three young children and a marriage to Jack that has sometimes been very difficult. Money is always in short supply, but with a little thought and invention Sarah makes sure there is always a treat at the end of every meal.

In addition to family puddings, this chapter features a few more exotic desserts from around the globe – from Italy and Australia courtesy of Marlon, Paris courtesy of Kelly and Roy. There are also two sensuous desserts, an exquisite choice from Chris and a homemade ice-cream from Bernice designed to get the pulses racing.

Chocolate Marquise with Crème Anglaise

Emmerdale's tastes are pretty sophisticated – even the Dingles have enjoyed special gourmet nights at the Woolpack and the old tearooms. Butch once tried to impress Mandy by taking her out for a gourmet dinner. She loved this classic partnership of chocolate and orange in a dark, seductive mousse, although it didn't have the romantic effect poor Butch desired – possibly because he spent the whole evening asking for chips and cans of bitter! Fine shreds of tangy orange zest compliment the bitter-sweetness of the chocolate in this dessert.

Alan's tip

This recipe is a food lover's delight. The ideal tin to use for this is what's called a 'moule à manqué', which has sides which slightly slope outwards. You can use an ordinary cake tin, but don't choose one with a loose base, or the mixture may leak through. Choose a really good quality plain chocolate for the finest flavour in this recipe – check on the label that it contains at least 70 per cent cocoa solids.

Serves 8

200g/7oz unsalted butter
200g/7oz caster sugar
350g/12oz plain dark
    continental chocolate
45ml/3 tablespoons brandy
5 medium eggs
finely grated zest of 1
    orange
45ml/3 tablespoons plain
    flour
curls of chocolate and
    orange zest strips for
    topping

SAUCE
500ml/18fl oz milk
1 vanilla pod
85g/3oz caster sugar
5 egg yolks
cocoa to sprinkle

1 Preheat the oven to 180°C/350°F/Gas 4. Butter a 23cm/9in round, deep cake tin and place a round of non-stick baking parchment in the base.

2 Place the butter and half the sugar in a pan and heat gently, without boiling, until dissolved. Remove from the heat and add the chocolate and brandy, stirring until melted and smooth.

3 Place the eggs, orange zest and remaining sugar in a bowl. Whisk until thick enough for the whisk to leave a trail in the mixture for a few seconds when lifted. Using a metal spoon, fold the chocolate mixture lightly and evenly into the egg mixture.

4 Sift the flour over the mixture, then fold in evenly with a metal spoon. Tip the mixture into the prepared tin. Place the tin in a roasting tin in the oven and pour in hot water to reach about half-way up the sides of the cake tin.

5 Bake in the oven for 50 minutes to 1 hour or until the marquise is just firm to the touch. Lift out of the roasting tin and leave to cool in its tin for about 30 minutes. To turn out, run a knife around the edge to loosen, then invert on to a serving plate. Decorate with curls of chocolate and strips of orange zest.

6 For the sauce, heat the milk in a small pan with the vanilla pod until just below boiling point. Remove from the heat and leave to stand for 10 minutes. Whisk the sugar and egg yolks together until smooth, then whisk the hot milk into this.

7 Return to the pan and cook gently, stirring constantly with a wooden spoon, until the mixture thickens slightly enough to coat the back of the spoon. Do not allow to boil. Leave to cool, then chill. Serve a little of the sauce in a pool around each slice of the marquise and sprinkle lightly with cocoa.

Antonia's Tiramisù

They say the way to a man's heart is through his stomach, and when that man is the most sophisticated of the Dingle clan, it's got to be something pretty special! Marlon first sampled this rich, seductive classic Italian dessert made by the lovely Antonia at the Bar Dinglesi in Venice. He immediately fell in love with it – and her.

Serves 6

15ml/1 tablespoon soft
   brown sugar
125ml/4fl oz hot, strong
   black coffee
2 medium eggs, separated
50g/1¾oz caster sugar
400g/14oz mascarpone
   cheese
45ml/3 tablespoons Marsala
   wine
175g/6oz plain sponge or
   Madeira cake
40g/1½oz amaretti
   biscuits, lightly crushed
100ml/3½fl oz Tia Maria
   liqueur
55g/2oz finely grated plain
   chocolate
15ml/1 tablespoon cocoa

1 Dissolve the brown sugar in the coffee and leave to cool completely.

2 Meanwhile, whisk the egg yolks with the caster sugar in a large bowl until thick and pale in colour. Beat in the mascarpone cheese and Marsala.

3 Whisk the egg whites in a clean, dry bowl until stiff enough to hold firm peaks. Fold lightly and evenly into the mascarpone mixture.

4 Crumble the sponge cake into a large serving bowl, or six individual dishes. Add the crumbled biscuits and sprinkle with the coffee and the Tia Maria.

5 Spoon half the mascarpone mixture over the sponge, smoothing evenly, then sprinkle with the grated chocolate. Top with the remaining mascarpone mix and smooth the top.

6 Sprinkle the top with cocoa and chill for at least 1 hour before serving.

Marlon's tip
For us well-travelled continental types, I suggest using Marsala, which gives a wonderful rich flavour to the dessert. Unfortunately you can't get it for love nor money in Viv Windsor's shop, so don't worry if you can't find it either. Just use the Tia Maria on its own.

Shrove Tuesday Pancakes

The annual village Pancake Dash on Shrove Tuesday every year is an event enjoyed by everyone in Emmerdale, especially the children. Pancakes are most commonly served simply – piping hot with a sprinkle of lemon juice and sugar – but these extra special citrus pancakes are a family treat from the Sugdens' kitchen.

Serves 4

100g/3½oz plain flour
pinch of salt
1 medium egg
300ml/½ pint milk and water, mixed
butter or oil for frying

FILLING
2 large oranges
15g/½oz butter
30ml/2 tablespoons clear honey
4 scoops vanilla ice-cream
freshly grated nutmeg to sprinkle

Sarah's tips for perfect pancakes Choose a good-quality, heavy-based small frying pan, but not too heavy or you'll have trouble tossing! If possible, keep your pan just for pancakes, as if you fry other foods in it your pancakes will stick. After use, simply wipe the pan clean with a soft, damp cloth or kitchen paper, never wash it or scour it, then your pancakes will never stick.

1 Sift the flour and salt into a bowl and make a well in the centre with the back of a spoon. Add the egg with a little of the milk and water and whisk until smooth, then add the remaining milk and whisk to a smooth, bubbly batter.

2 Heat a small amount of butter or oil in a small, heavy-based frying pan. Pour in a little batter and quickly swirl evenly over the pan. Cook until the underneath is golden brown.

3 Either toss or turn the pancake, then cook over a moderate heat until the second side is golden brown. Remove and cook the remaining batter in the same way, making about 8 pancakes. Interleave with non-stick baking parchment and keep hot.

4 Remove a few shreds of orange zest for decoration then cut all the pith and peel from the orange. Use a sharp knife to remove the segments, catching the juice in a bowl.

5 Melt the butter in a pan and add the honey and orange juice. Allow to bubble for 1 minute, then add the orange segments.

6 Fold the pancakes into quarters and fill with orange segments. Spoon over the juice from the pan and top with scoops of ice-cream. Sprinkle with nutmeg and serve immediately.

Apple and Cheese Pie

There's an old Yorkshire saying that 'Apple pie without the cheese is like a kiss without a squeeze', and it's traditional to eat a piece of young white cheese such as Wensleydale with apple pie. This recipe bakes tasty little chunks of cheese in the pie with the apple filling, which makes it meltingly delicious – a perfect dish for courting couples like Butch and Emily.

Serves 6

250g/9oz plain flour
pinch of salt
125g/4½oz butter
cold water to mix
800g/1lb 12oz Bramley
    apples
75g/2¾oz caster sugar
2.5ml/½ teaspoon ground
    cinnamon
finely grated zest and juice
    of ½ a lemon
85g/3oz Wensleydale
    cheese, diced
milk and caster sugar for
    glazing

1 Preheat the oven to 190°C/375°F/Gas Mark 5. Sift the flour and salt into a bowl and rub in the butter until it resembles fine breadcrumbs.

2 Stir in just enough water to mix to a firm dough. Roll out about half of the pastry on a lightly floured surface and use to line a 23cm/9in round deep pie plate.

3 Peel, core and slice the apples. Toss the slices with the sugar, cinnamon, lemon zest and juice. Spread half the apple into the pastry-lined dish and scatter with the cheese. Top with the remaining apples, spreading evenly.

4 Roll out the remaining pastry to make a lid for the pie, sealing the edges with water. Trim the edges with a sharp knife and pinch the pastry edges between finger and thumb to decorate. Cut a small hole in the top for steam to escape.

5 Decorate with pastry trimmings, brush with milk to glaze and sprinkle lightly with caster sugar. Place on a baking sheet and bake for 35–40 minutes or until golden brown. Serve warm.

Betty's tip
It's heresy to say this in Yorkshire, but if you can't get Wensleydale cheese, try using Lancashire instead, which makes a good substitute.

Seth's Raspberry Tipsy Pudding

A lavish, old-fashioned pudding that resembles a rich, boozy trifle – Seth can't resist it! He uses the expensive brandy given to him by Kim Tate, Emmerdale's most infamous fugitive from justice. Seth and Kim were always close friends, and this pudding is a unique way to make a toast to absent friends.

Serves 4

200g/7oz Madeira cake or
    plain sponge cake
75g/2¾oz fresh or frozen
    raspberries
60ml/4 tablespoons
    shredless marmalade
15ml/1 tablespoon icing
    sugar
30ml/2 tablespoons brandy
40g/1½oz macaroon
    biscuits
100ml/3½fl oz medium-dry
    sherry
200ml/7fl oz double cream
whole raspberries and fresh
    mint leaves to decorate

1 Crumble the sponge cake and place in a glass dish or pudding basin with the raspberries.

2 Place the marmalade, icing sugar and brandy in a pan and heat gently until melted. Drizzle over the sponge, making sure it is well distributed.

3 Crumble the macaroons lightly and sprinkle over the sponge, then sprinkle with the sherry. Chill for at least 2 hours.

4 Whip the cream until it just begins to hold its shape, then spread evenly over the top. Decorate with raspberries and mint leaves and serve.

Seth's tip
There's nowt wrong with a big dollop of double cream, but Betty sometimes brings home fromage frais or Greek-style yoghurt from the diner when she's watching her figure.

Passionfruit and Strawberry Ice-cream

Bernice's romantic evenings are always carefully planned down to the last detail so she and Gavin can get in the mood for love. Silky-smooth and creamy in texture, this unusual ice-cream combines the exotic flavour of passionfruit with juicy strawberries to make an irresistibly seductive dish for them to tuck into late at night, after the pub closes.

Serves 6
Makes about 1 litre/1¾ pints

2 medium eggs
100g/3½oz caster sugar
300ml/½ pint milk
225g/8oz fresh
    strawberries, hulled
300ml/½ pint crème fraîche
2 large passionfruit

Bernice's tip

Unless you plan to serve the ice-cream all at once, or you're not concerned about fitting into your hipsters, it's a good idea to freeze it in small batches. Better still, freeze it in separate scoops, so you can remove just enough for two!

1 Place the eggs and sugar in a large bowl and whisk until pale and frothy. Heat the milk until almost boiling, then whisk into the egg mixture.

2 Place the bowl over a pan of simmering water and stir constantly until the mixture is slightly thickened. Cool completely and chill in the refrigerator.

3 Purée the strawberries in a food processor or blender. Halve the passionfruit and scoop out the flesh, then stir into the purée. Stir together the chilled custard, fruit purée and crème fraîche.

4 Tip into an ice-cream maker and churn for about 20 minutes, or according to manufacturer's instructions. Alternatively, tip into a freezer container, freeze for about 1 hour and whisk hard to break up the ice crystals, then repeat the freezing and whisking once more.

5 Store the ice-cream in a tightly sealed freezer container in the freezer for up to 1 month. To serve, allow the ice-cream to stand at room temperature for 10–15 minutes before serving in scoops, with fresh strawberries.

Bernice made it her aim to add an air of sophistication when she took over the Woolpack – much to Tricia's annoyance!

Sticky-topped Ginger Pudding

As busy working parents, Angie and Sean have little time for complicated cooking, so puddings don't regularly feature on the Reynolds' dinner table. But this one is made and cooked in less than 5 minutes, and it's simple enough for anyone in the family to make.

Serves 4

115g/4oz soft margarine
30ml/2 tablespoons ginger preserve
100g/3½oz golden caster sugar
100g/3½oz self-raising flour
5ml/1 teaspoon ground ginger
2 medium eggs

1 Use 15g/½oz of the margarine to grease a 1.2 litre/2 pint pudding basin. Spoon in the ginger preserve.

2 Place all the remaining ingredients in a bowl and beat well until evenly mixed. Spoon into the basin and cover with a microwave-proof plate or pierced clingfilm.

3 Cook in the microwave on High(100% power) for 4 minutes, then leave to stand for 1 minute. Turn out on to a serving plate and serve hot, with Greek-style yogurt or custard.

Angie's tip

Most supermarkets have jars of ginger preserve – look in the jams section. If you can't find it, spoon in a tablespoon of golden syrup and a tablespoon of chopped glacé ginger instead.

Blueberry and Lemon Cheesecake

A light, tangy cheesecake which is very simple to make and can be baked a day in advance. When blueberries are not in season you can substitute other soft fruits, such as raspberries or blackberries. Jack likes it served with a large pouring of cream after a hard day's work.

Serves 6

50g/1¾oz butter
115g/4oz gingernut biscuits, crushed
3 lemons
250g/9oz ricotta cheese
175g/6oz Greek-style yogurt
3 large eggs
15ml/1 tablespoon cornflour
75g/2¾oz caster sugar
125g/4½oz fresh or frozen blueberries
icing sugar to sprinkle

1 Preheat the oven to 180°C/350°F/Gas Mark 4. Melt the butter and stir in the biscuit crumbs. Press into the base of a lightly greased 20cm/8in loose-bottomed cake tin on a baking sheet. Bake for 10 minutes.

2 Remove a few slices of lemon for decoration and reserve. Finely grate the zest and squeeze the juice from the rest. Add the ricotta, yogurt, eggs, cornflour and sugar and whisk until smooth. Stir the blueberries into the mixture.

3 Spoon the mixture into the tin and smooth the surface level. Bake in the oven for about 40–45 minutes, or until just firm and golden brown. Cool the cheesecake completely in the tin, then run a knife around the edge to loosen and turn out on to a serving plate.

4 To serve, decorate with the reserved lemon slices, then sprinkle with icing sugar.

Kathy's tip
Don't worry if the cheesecake splits on top as it cools, it's meant to – it's just the nature of the beast!

Lavish Lime and Coconut Roulade

Chris may not be the nicest guy in Emmerdale, but he certainly knows how to impress a woman with a romantic meal at an expensive restaurant. It's usually his personality that ruins the date. But who could resist this luxurious, marshmallow texture and creamy-smooth lime and coconut filling with a seductive kick of Cointreau?

Serves 4–6

3 large egg whites
175g/6oz caster sugar
5ml/1 teaspoon cornflour
5ml/1 teaspoon vinegar
30ml/2 tablespoons
    desiccated coconut,
    toasted

FILLING
finely grated zest of 1 lime
200g/7oz Greek yogurt
20g/¾oz creamed coconut,
    finely grated
20ml/4 teaspoons Cointreau
lime slices and curls of
    coconut to decorate

1 Preheat the oven to 140°C/275°F/Gas Mark 1. Line a 23 x 33cm/9 x 13in Swiss roll tin with non-stick paper.

2 Place the egg whites in a clean, grease-free bowl and whisk until stiff. Whisk in about half the sugar, a tablespoon at a time. Whisk in the cornflour and vinegar, then add the remaining sugar and whisk until the mixture resembles marshmallow.

3 Spoon into the prepared tin and smooth level. Sprinkle with the desiccated coconut. Bake in the oven for 35–40 minutes, or until firm to the touch. Cover loosely with a large piece of foil and leave to cool completely.

4 When the meringue is cool, turn it out on to a sheet of paper lightly sprinkled with toasted coconut.

5 Stir the lime zest into the yogurt with the coconut cream and Cointreau. Spread the filling evenly over the meringue to within 1cm/½in of the edges.

6 Using the paper to support it, roll up the meringue from one short edge with the filling inside. Decorate with lime slices and curls of coconut.

Chris's tip
I find Cointreau the best liqueur to use, but try it with Grand Marnier – it's equally seductive!

Chris went to extraordinary lengths to try to win Kathy back. He booked an intimate dinner at the hotel where he and Kathy had spent their wedding night – and then he sabotaged his car in the hope that they would have to stay overnight. Unluckily for Chris, Kathy saw right through his plan.

Down-under Pavlova with Tropical Fruits

The Dingles didn't have much in the way of fancy food in Australia, but this dish is one down-under speciality they just couldn't resist. The Australians serve it lavishly topped with cream and lots of colourful, fresh tropical fruit, but you can vary the fruits depending on the season.

Serves 8

4 medium egg whites
200g/7oz caster sugar
10ml/2 teaspoons cornflour
10ml/2 teaspoons white
   wine vinegar
5ml/1 teaspoon vanilla
   essence

TOPPING
300ml/½ pint double cream
1 pawpaw
1 mango
2 kiwifruit
2 passionfruit

Mandy's tip
You could make a right pig's ear of this if you're not careful. If you're worried about moving the meringue on to a serving platter, make it easy on yourself by baking it in a shallow ovenproof dish instead – or a flat ovenproof pizza plate is ideal. Omit the non-stick paper and butter the dish instead.

1 Preheat the oven to 120°C/250°F/Gas Mark ½. Line a large baking sheet with non-stick paper. Place the egg whites in a large, clean bowl and whisk hard until stiff and standing in peaks.

2 Gradually whisk in the sugar about a third at a time, whisking hard until the mixture is very stiff and shiny. Whisk in the cornflour, vinegar and vanilla.

3 Spread the meringue on to the baking paper in a round shape about 25cm/10in wide. Make a wide hollow in the centre for the topping.

4 Bake for about 1 hour 15 minutes to 1 hour 30 minutes, until crisp and slightly browned, but still slightly soft in the centre. Remove from the oven and cool completely. The meringue may crack at this stage.

5 Whip the cream until it just holds its shape, then spoon into the hollow centre of the meringue.

6 Halve, peel and de-seed the pawpaw, peel and stone the mango and peel the kiwifruit. Chop the fruit into bite-sized chunks, then arrange over the pavlova. Halve the passionfruit and spoon the flesh over the fruits.

Crème Brûlee aux Cerises

Kelly and Roy's indulgent honeymoon in Paris, courtesy of Chris Tate's wallet, gave them a chance to try a few classic French dishes at their finest, and this is perhaps one of the most memorable – a luxurious crème brûlée with cherries.

Serves 6

600ml/1 pint double cream
1 vanilla pod
6 egg yolks
125g/4½oz caster sugar
5ml/1 teaspoon cornflour
300g/10½oz fresh cherries, pitted
15ml/1 tablespoon kirsch (optional)

Kelly's tip

As usual, when I'm trying to make something nice for Roy, Viv never stocks any useful ingredients. Mind you, if you use vanilla essence instead of a vanilla pod it's pretty simple. You'll need about 2.5ml/½ teaspoon of essence, and there's no need to leave the cream to stand – just add the essence and pour it straight on to the egg yolk mixture. Also, it's OK to use canned cherries if there are no fresh ones available. Roy won't notice the difference anyway.

1 Pour the cream into a heavy-based saucepan and add the vanilla pod. Place over a moderate heat until almost boiling. Remove from the heat, cover and leave to infuse for 30 minutes. Remove the vanilla pod.

2 Whisk the egg yolks with 30ml/2 tablespoons of the sugar and the cornflour in a large bowl. Pour on the hot cream, stirring constantly to mix evenly.

3 Pour the custard back into the pan and heat very gently, stirring continuously with a wooden spoon for about 20 minutes, or until the mixture thickens enough to just coat the back of the spoon. Remove from the heat.

4 Halve the cherries, toss with the kirsch, then divide between 6 small ramekins or flameproof dishes. Strain the custard over, filling almost to the top. Leave to cool, then cover with clingfilm and chill in the refrigerator for several hours until set.

5 Preheat a grill to very hot. Sprinkle the remaining sugar in a thick, even layer over each dish. Place under the grill very close to the heat, or use a blowtorch to caramelize the tops to a rich, glossy toffee. Cool, then chill before serving.

Marmalade Bread and Butter Pudding

This quick, economical pudding makes regular appearances on the Sugdens' dinner table. Sarah uses up yesterday's leftover bread with whatever dried fruits she has in the store-cupboard.

Serves 6

55g/2oz unsalted butter
6 thick slices white bread
60ml/4 tablespoons
    marmalade
100g/3½oz mixed dried
    fruits
3 medium eggs
700ml/1¼ pints milk
10ml/2 teaspoons demerara
    sugar
5ml/1 teaspoon ground
    mixed spice

1 Preheat the oven to 180°C/350°F/Gas Mark 4. Use a little of the measured butter to grease a 1.7 litre/3 pint shallow ovenproof dish. Spread the remainder over the bread slices, then spread with marmalade and cut into triangles.

2 Arrange the bread slices in the prepared dish, sprinkling the fruit between the slices. Beat the eggs and milk and pour evenly over the bread. If possible, leave the dish to stand for about 15 minutes for the custard to soak into the bread.

3 Sprinkle the demerara sugar and spice over the pudding. Bake in the oven for 40–50 minutes, or until the pudding is lightly set and golden brown. Serve warm, either on its own, or with a spoonful of natural yogurt.

Sarah's tip
I'm always busy on the farm, so when I have a spare moment I like to get things done. I can make this pudding early in the day, then store it in the fridge ready to pop in the oven when Jack and the kids come home hungry.

Teas, Cakes and Bakes

Summer cricket matches are an institution in Emmerdale and the cricket pavilion has seen some historic battles over the years, notably the competition for the Butterworth Ball. Butterworth was a local shepherd who was passing through the village in July 1891 when Beckindale (as Emmerdale was then known) was playing Robblesfield. The Beckindale team were a man short, and Butterworth agreed to play on their side. He won the game for them, hitting the ball over a quarter of a mile! It became a tradition for the two villages to play for the ball every year.

Cricket matches are a great way of settling old scores. The village used to field a team against NY Estates who ran Home Farm. Nowadays the teams represent the Woolpack and the Malt Shovel, and also hold an annual rugby match. The 1999 Woolpack team were a sorry bunch, it must be said. Even Seth fell asleep whilst on umpiring duty! Luckily Emily Wylie deputised for Seth, and her encyclopaedic knowledge of the rules of the game ensured that the Woolpack won the day. This was a great relief for Alan, as it had been agreed that the losers were to pay for the evening's liquid refreshment! Of course, no summer cricket match is complete without a great cricket tea. These are tried and tested recipes that taste just as good today as in 1891!

Summertime attracts walkers and other tourists to the Dales, and the diner tempts many with its great array of cakes. With Betty and Sarah on hand to offer help and advice, how could it fail! There's nothing better than a good slice of cake, a cup of strong Yorkshire tea, and a breath of fresh country air. Bear in mind Betty's warning though – one too many slices and it'll go straight to your hips!

Marlon and Betty were not convinced that making croissants was suitable therapy for Kathy after she discharged herself from hospital, but she was desperate to get back to work. Even croissants appeared more stimulating than weeks of jigsaw puzzles!

Angel Food Cake with Pineapple

It's important for Alan to watch his weight, but he's always on the lookout for recipes that will allow him treats without breaking the rules, or getting an earful from Tricia and Bernice! This one is virtually fat-free, so he can take a slice with a clear conscience.

Serves 8

50g/1¾oz ready-to-eat
   sweetened dried
   pineapple
115g/4oz plain flour
8 large egg whites
1.25ml/¼ teaspoon salt
5ml/1 teaspoon cream of
   tartar
5ml/1 teaspoon almond
   essence
250g/9oz caster sugar

1 Preheat the oven to 170°C/325°F/Gas Mark 3. Brush the inside of a 1.7 litre/3 pint ring tin with oil. Finely chop the pineapple and mix with 15ml/1 tablespoon of the flour.

2 Whisk the egg whites in a large, clean bowl to a soft foam. Add the salt and cream of tartar and whisk until stiff but not dry.

3 Whisk in the almond essence, then add the sugar, a tablespoon at a time, whisking hard between each addition.

4 Sift the remaining flour over the mixture and fold in lightly and evenly with a metal spoon, then fold in the pineapple.

5 Spoon the mixture into the prepared tin and bake in the oven for 40–45 minutes, or until the cake is golden brown and firm to the touch.

6 Turn the tin upside down on a wire rack but do not turn out the cake. Leave to cool, then run a knife around the edge and turn out the cake.

Alan's tip

This cake is good just as it is, but is even more delicious served with a spoonful of low-fat crème fraîche on the side.

Dales Cut-and-Come-Again Cake

This light, simple fruit cake has long been a favourite at Emmerdale Farm, as it keeps well for about a month. With all the comings and goings at the Sugdens, even if someone takes out a slice and puts the rest back for later, the cake stays moist and tasty for next time.

Serves 10–12

250g/9oz mixed dried fruit
30ml/2 tablespoons sherry
   or lemon juice
250g/9oz butter or
   margarine
200g/7oz caster sugar
3 medium eggs, beaten
45ml/3 tablespoons golden
   syrup
250g/9oz self-raising flour
30ml/2 tablespoons cocoa

1 Preheat the oven to 170°C/325°F/Gas Mark 3. Grease and line a deep, 20cm/8in diameter round cake tin. Place the fruit in a bowl and stir in the sherry or lemon juice.

2 Cream the butter or margarine with the sugar until pale in colour and fluffy in texture. Gradually add the eggs to the mixture, beating thoroughly after each addition.

3 Stir in the golden syrup and fruit mixture, mixing evenly. Sift the flour and cocoa into the mix, and fold in lightly and evenly.

4 Spoon the mixture into the prepared tin and smooth the surface. Bake in the oven for about 1¼–2 hours.

5 Cool slightly in the tin, then turn out and finish cooling on a wire rack. Cool completely before storage.

Sarah's tip

This is a tip I learnt from Annie. For best results, store the cake in an ordinary biscuit tin, or wrap it closely in foil, preferably not in a polythene container.

Yorkshire Fat Rascals

Betty updated these little scone-like pastries for the diner from an old Yorkshire recipe. In some parts they are cooked on a flat griddle, but these days they're more commonly cooked in a hot oven. Perfect for rascals of all ages!

Makes 16

400g/14oz plain flour
1.25ml/¼ teaspoon salt
2.5ml/½ teaspoon grated
   nutmeg
10ml/2 teaspoons baking
   powder
175g/6oz butter or
   margarine
75g/2¾oz golden caster
   sugar
85g/3oz currants
40g/1½oz glace cherries,
   chopped
100-125ml/3½–4½fl oz single
   cream and milk, mixed

1 Preheat the oven to 220°C/425°F/Gas Mark 7. Sift the flour, salt, nutmeg and baking powder into a bowl.

2 Rub the butter or margarine into the flour until the mixture looks like fine breadcrumbs. Stir in the sugar, currants, cherries and just enough cream and milk to make a soft dough.

3 Roll out the dough on a lightly floured surface to about 2.5cm/1in thick. Cut into 5cm/2in rounds and place on a lightly greased baking sheet.

4 Brush lightly with milk to glaze and bake in the oven for 15–20 minutes, until lightly browned. Cool on a wire rack.

Betty's tip
These little cakes are best eaten very fresh on the day of making – even better when still slightly warm from the oven. My Seth loves them, as he'll never get told off for eating them without permission!

Rhubarb Streusel Cake

Yorkshire rhubarb is thought to be the best in England, and Seth's carefully tended rhubarb patch provides the finest tangy-sweet fruit for these delicious crumbly slices. It's also very good made with gooseberries.

Makes 8 slices

500g/1lb 2oz rhubarb
225g/8oz self-raising flour
175g/6oz unsalted butter
150g/5½oz golden caster sugar
60g/2¼oz ground hazelnuts
finely grated zest of 1 small orange
1 medium egg, beaten
5ml/1 teaspoon cornflour
15ml/1 tablespoon chopped glacé ginger
30ml/2 tablespoons orange juice

1 Preheat the oven to 180°C/350°F/Gas Mark 4. Trim the rhubarb and cut into 2cm/¾in thick slices.

2 Sift the flour and rub in the butter (you can do this in a food processor if you prefer). Stir in the sugar, hazelnuts and orange zest.

3 Reserve 175g/6oz of the mixture and add the egg to the remainder. Mix to a fairly soft dough. Using the back of a spoon, press the dough into the base and halfway up the sides of a 23cm/9in diameter spring-release tin.

4 Stir together the rhubarb, cornflour, ginger and orange juice, then tip into the dough-lined tin, spreading evenly. Spoon the crumble mixture evenly over the rhubarb.

5 Bake in the oven for 40–45 minutes or until firm and golden brown. Cool in the tin, then run a knife around the edge and turn out. Sprinkle with icing sugar and cut into slices to serve.

Betty's tip
If you find it hard to buy ground hazelnuts, you can grind whole, blanched hazelnuts in a food processor. Alternatively, use ground almonds instead.

Old Peculiar Fruit Cake

This rich, dark, deep fruit cake, enriched with pecan nuts and Old Peculiar Ale, is a staple of the diner's cake menu. It's best stored for at least a week before eating.

Makes one 1 cake (8 slices)

125g/4½oz pecan nuts
200g/7oz ready-to-eat
   prunes
400g/14oz plain flour
7.5ml/1½ teaspoons ground
   mixed spice
200g/7oz unsalted butter
325g/11½oz light
   muscovado sugar
100g/3½oz seedless raisins
100g/3½oz chopped mixed
   peel
finely grated zest of ½ a
   lemon
3 medium eggs
250ml/9fl oz Old Peculiar
   Ale
5ml/1 teaspoon bicarbonate
   of soda

1 Preheat the oven to 170°C/325°F/Gas Mark 3. Grease and line a 20cm/8in round deep cake tin. Reserve 16 pecan halves for decoration and chop the rest. Roughly chop the prunes.

2 Sift the flour and spice into a bowl, then rub in the butter until the mixture resembles fine breadcrumbs (you can do this very quickly in a food processor). Stir in the sugar, then add the chopped pecans, prunes, sultanas, peel and lemon zest, mixing thoroughly.

3 Lightly whisk the eggs with the ale and bicarbonate of soda, mixing evenly. Stir thoroughly into the dry ingredients to make a fairly soft consistency.

4 Spoon the mixture into the cake tin and spread the surface level. Arrange the reserved pecan nuts on top. Bake in the oven for 1½–1¾ hours, until the cake is firm and beginning to shrink from the sides of the tin. Cool in the tin for 30 minutes, then turn out and finish cooling on a wire rack.

Kathy's tip
We use Old Peculiar Ale in the diner, but you can use another traditional dark brown ale instead.

Double Chocolate Chip American Brownies

These super-rich, gooey little brownies are a popular choice with the ladies at Kathy's Diner – they're great with a cappuccino coffee for a mid-morning gossip.

Makes 12–16 squares

115g/4oz plain dark
   chocolate
2 medium eggs
200g/7oz light muscovado
   sugar
100ml/3½fl oz sunflower oil
5ml/1 teaspoon vanilla
   essence
50g/1¾oz self-raising flour
2.5ml/½ teaspoon baking
   powder
60ml/4 tablespoons cocoa
   powder
50g/1¾oz chopped
   walnuts
50g/1¾oz white chocolate
   chips

1 Preheat the oven to 180°C/350°F/Gas 4. Lightly grease a 19cm/7½in square shallow cake tin.

2 Break up the chocolate and place in a bowl over a pan of hot water. Heat gently until the chocolate is just melted.

3 Beat the eggs in a large bowl with the sugar, oil and vanilla, then add the chocolate and beat to mix evenly.

4 Sift the flour, baking powder and cocoa together and fold into the chocolate mixture with the chopped nuts and chocolate chips. Tip the mixture into the prepared tin and spread evenly.

5 Bake for 30–35 minutes, or until the top is just firm. Cool in the tin before cutting into 12–16 squares.

Kathy's tip
These brownies are best served freshly made, but they will freeze successfully for up to three months. Pack into an airtight container for freezing, and thaw at room temperature.

Cheese and Chive Scone Wedges

These go down a treat at village cricket teas and summer fairs, and they're very easy to make.

Makes 8

225g/8oz self-raising flour
pinch of salt
5ml/1 teaspoon baking
  powder
5ml/1 teaspoon wholegrain
  mustard powder
40g/1½oz butter or
  margarine
75g/2¾oz finely grated
  Cheddar cheese
approx 150ml/¼ pint milk
milk to glaze
200g/7oz cream cheese with
  chives

1 Preheat the oven to 220°C/425°F/Gas Mark 7. Lightly grease a baking sheet. Sift the flour, salt and baking powder into a bowl.

2 Rub in the butter or margarine evenly with your fingertips until the mixture resembles fine breadcrumbs. Stir in 55g/2oz Cheddar and the wholegrain mustard, then add just enough milk to mix to a fairly soft dough.

3 Turn out the dough on a lightly floured surface and press into a large, smooth round, about 2.5cm/1in thick. Lift on to the baking sheet and use a sharp knife to mark into 8 wedges, cutting deeply but not right through.

4 Brush with a little milk to glaze and sprinkle with the remaining Cheddar. Bake in the oven for 15–20 minutes, or until well-risen, firm and golden brown. Cool on a wire rack.

5 When the scone round is cool, cut into 8 wedges and split each wedge across in half. Spread with cream cheese and sandwich back together to serve.

Kathy found that three was a crowd when Eric employed Mandy as the new wine bar chef!

Marlon's Death by Chocolate Cake

Mandy is a true chocoholic and can't resist a slice of this, the richest chocolate cake Marlon ever made. She'd prefer to scoff the whole lot herself but it's big enough to share with the whole of the Dingle clan!

Marlon's tip

Here's a tip for added *savoir faire*. The easiest way to make chocolate curls is to take a bar of chocolate at room temperature and with a vegetable peeler shave curls of chocolate from the sides of the bar. *Voila*!

Serves 16

225g/8oz self-raising flour
5ml/1 teaspoon baking
    powder
5ml/1 teaspoon cinnamon
225g/8oz plain dark
    chocolate
150ml/¼ pint milk
115g/4 oz unsalted butter
200g/7oz light muscovado
    sugar
10ml/2 teaspoons vanilla
    essence
2 egg whites
3 egg yolks
100ml/3½fl oz soured cream

FILLING
75g/2¾oz seedless
    raspberry jam
75ml/5 tablespoons dark
    rum
350g/12oz plain dark
    chocolate
175g/6oz unsalted butter

FROSTING
250g/9oz plain dark
    chocolate
250ml/9fl oz double cream

TO DECORATE
chocolate curls

1 Preheat the oven to 180°C/350°F/Gas Mark 4. Grease a 23cm/9in diameter spring-release cake tin and line the base and sides with non-stick baking parchment. Sift together the flour, baking powder and cinnamon.

2 Break up the chocolate and place in a pan with the milk and butter. Stir over a low heat until just melted, but do not allow to boil. Remove from the heat and stir in the sugar and vanilla. Allow to cool slightly.

3 Whisk the egg whites in a clean dry bowl until stiff. Beat together the egg yolks and soured cream, then beat quickly into the chocolate mixture. Fold in the flour mixture lightly and evenly. Quickly fold in the egg whites, then tip the mixture into the prepared tin.

4 Bake for 45–55 minutes, or until well-risen and firm to the touch. Cool in the tin for 10 minutes, then turn out on to a wire rack and leave until completely cool.

5 Split the cake crosswise into 3 layers. Warm the raspberry jam gently with 45ml/3 tablespoons of rum until melted and brush evenly over the cakes.

6 Place the remaining rum in a pan with the chocolate and butter. Heat gently, stirring, until melted and smooth. Cool slightly, then spread half the mixture over the bottom layer of cake. Top with another layer of cake, jam side up, and spread with the rest of the chocolate filling. Top with another layer of cake, pressing down lightly.

7 For the frosting, break up the chocolate and place in a pan with the cream. Heat gently without boiling, stirring until melted, then remove from the heat. Beat until it is just cool enough to hold its shape. Spread the frosting over the top and sides of the cake. Decorate with chocolate curls.

Passion Cake

This cake is an enduring favourite with visitors to the Dales. Instead of a plain traditional cream-cheese frosting, Kathy serves this light, fruity carrot cake with an irresistibly rich passionfruit frosting lavishly swirled over the surface.

Makes 1 cake, 8 slices

225g/8oz carrots
40g/1½oz walnut pieces
5 medium eggs
150g/5½oz light brown
    muscovado sugar
175g/6oz plain flour
5ml/1 teaspoon ground
    cinnamon
75g/2¾oz sultanas
finely grated zest of 1 small
    orange

FROSTING
2 passionfruit
250g/9oz mascarpone
    cheese
30ml/2 tablespoons icing
    sugar

1 Preheat the oven to 190°C/375°F/Gas Mark 5. Grease and line a 20cm/8in round deep cake tin. Peel and grate the carrots on a medium grater. Roughly chop the walnuts.

2 Place the eggs and sugar in a large bowl and whisk over a pan of hot water until very thick and mousse-like. The whisk should leave a trail for a few seconds when lifted.

3 Sift the flour and cinnamon over the mixture and fold in lightly and evenly, using a metal spoon. Fold in the carrots, walnuts, sultanas and orange zest.

4 Pour into the prepared tin and bake in the oven for 40–45 minutes, or until golden brown, well-risen and springy to the touch. Cool for a few minutes in the tin, then finish cooling on a wire rack.

5 For the frosting, halve the passionfruit and scoop out the flesh into a bowl. Add the mascarpone and icing sugar and mix until smooth. Split the cake horizontally into 3 layers. Use about a third of the frosting to sandwich the layers together, then spread the remainder over the top, swirling with a palette knife.

Kathy's tip
If you prefer not to have the passionfruit pips in the frosting, just press the flesh through a sieve to remove the seeds before adding the juicy pulp to the mascarpone.

Date and Walnut Teabread

It was said that Sarah could burn water when she first came to live at Emmerdale, but her baking improved no end after a couple of lessons from Annie. Nowadays at village cricket teas Sarah serves this simple homely teabread sliced and buttered, but it's also very good on its own. She makes it with good strong Yorkshire tea, but for a more unusual flavour you could use a scented tea such as Earl Grey.

Makes 1 large loaf

200g/7oz stoned dates,
    chopped
5ml/1 teaspoon bicarbonate
    of soda
finely grated rind of 1
    lemon
200ml/7fl oz hot tea
75g/2¾oz soft margarine
175g/6oz light muscovado
    sugar
1 medium egg
200g/7oz self-raising flour
60g/2¼oz walnuts,
    chopped

1 Preheat the oven to 180°C/350°F/Gas Mark 4. Grease a 19 x 12.5cm/7½ x 4½in loaf tin and line the base with non-stick paper.

2 Place the dates, bicarbonate of soda and lemon rind in a bowl and add the hot tea. Leave to soak for 10 minutes until softened.

3 Beat together the margarine, sugar and egg. Stir in the date mixture. Fold in the flour, mixing thoroughly, then fold in the walnuts. Spoon the mixture into the tin and spread evenly.

4 Bake for 50 minutes to 1 hour or until risen, firm and golden brown. Cool for 10 minutes in the tin, then turn out and finish cooling on a wire rack. Serve in slices, spread with butter.

Sarah's tip
This cake freezes well for up to 3 months. It's a good idea to cut it into slices and interleave each slice with a sheet of non-stick paper, then overwrap and freeze. This way, when Angie comes round for a gossip, I can remove just one or two slices for a treat with our coffee, without having to wait for the whole cake to defrost.

Betty's Never-fail Victoria Sponge Cake

Betty is known for her prize-winning cakes, and this classic recipe is a regular winner at the village summer fair. 'I'd put my Victoria Sponge against any in Yorkshire, bar none,' she says. It's filled with her homemade lemon curd, but you can use ordinary jam if you prefer.

Makes 1 cake (8 slices)

175g/6oz unsalted butter, at
    room temperature
175g/6oz golden caster
    sugar
finely grated zest of 1
    lemon
3 medium eggs
175g/6oz self-raising flour

TO FINISH
75ml/5 tablespoons lemon
    curd (preferably home-
    made)
icing sugar to sprinkle

1 Preheat the oven to 190°C/375°F/Gas mark 5. Grease two 18cm/7in sandwich tins and line the base of each with a round of non-stick baking paper.

2 Place the butter in a bowl and beat hard with an electric mixer until softened. Add the sugar and lemon zest and whisk together until pale in colour and fluffy in texture.

3 Beat the eggs together and gradually add to the mixture, beating hard between each addition. Sift half the flour over the mix and fold in lightly and evenly with a metal spoon. Fold in the remaining flour.

4 Divide the mixture between the tins and smooth the surface level. Bake in the oven for 20–25 minutes, or until the cakes are well-risen and spring back when pressed lightly.

5 Turn out the cakes on to a wire rack and leave to cool completely. Sandwich together with the lemon curd or jam and sprinkle with icing sugar to finish.

Betty's tip
For a midsummer treat, add a few slices of strawberries to the filling before sandwiching the cakes together.

Kathy and Biff dressed up as Sandy and Danny from Grease *for the Woolpack Hollywood night. Biff hoped it would be a night to remember, but Kathy was mortified when he presented her with a heart-shaped cake inscribed with a marriage proposal! Betty, on the other hand, thought it was a lovely gesture, and declared, 'I'd be on cloud nine if a man asked for my hand with the aid of a dedicated sponge.'*

Index